The Best
AMERICAN
FOOD
WRITING
2023

T0005645

GUEST EDITORS OF THE BEST AMERICAN FOOD WRITING

2018–RUTH REICHL
2019–SAMIN NOSRAT
2020–J. KENJI LÓPEZ-ALT
2021–GABRIELLE HAMILTON
2022–SOHLA EL-WAYLLY
2023–MARK BITTMAN

The Best AMERICAN FOOD WRITING™ 2023

Edited and with an Introduction
by MARK BITTMAN

SILVIA KILLINGSWORTH, Series Editor

MARINER BOOKS
New York   Boston

THE BEST AMERICAN FOOD WRITING™. Copyright © 2023 by HarperCollins Publishers LLC. Introduction copyright © 2023 by Mark Bittman. Foreword copyright © 2023 by Silvia Killingsworth. The Best American Series® is a registered trademark of HarperCollins Publishers LLC. *The Best American Food Writing*™ is a trademark of HarperCollins Publishers LLC. All rights reserved. Printed in the United States of America. No part of this book may be used or reproduced in any manner whatsoever without written permission except in the case of brief quotations embodied in critical articles and reviews. HarperCollins Publishers LLC is not authorized to grant permission for further uses of copyrighted selections reprinted in this book without the permission of their owners. Permission must be obtained from the individual copyright owners as identified herein. For information, address HarperCollins Publishers, 195 Broadway, New York, NY 10007

HarperCollins books may be purchased for educational, business, or sales promotional use. For information, please email the Special Markets Department at SPsales@harpercollins.com.

FIRST EDITION

ISSN 2578-7667
ISBN 978-0-06-332252-3

23 24 25 26 27 LBC 6 5 4 3 2

"Black Farmers in Arkansas Still Seek Justice a Century After the Elaine Massacre" by Wesley Brown. First published in *Civil Eats*, July 27, 2022. Copyright © 2022 by Wesley Brown. Reprinted by permission of the author.

"Detroit's Chinatown and Gayborhood Felt Like Two Separate Worlds. Then They Collided" by Curtis Chin. First published in *Bon Appétit*, June 22, 2022. Copyright © 2022 by Curtis Chin. Reprinted by permission of the author.

"Tales of an Accidental Cooking Club" by Mike Diago. First published in *The Bittman Project*, September 8, 2022. Copyright © 2022 by Mike Diago. Reprinted by permission of the author.

"Kimchi with a Side of Whale" by Jennifer Fergesen. First published in *Eater*, July 13, 2022. Copyright © 2022 by Vox Media, LLC. Reprinted by permission of Vox Media, LLC.

"On the Road, a Taste of Home" by Madhushree Ghosh. First published in *High Country News*, September 1, 2022. Copyright © 2022 by Madhushree Ghosh. Reprinted by permission of the author.

"My Year in Review as Free Press Restaurant Critic: Accidentally Anonymous" by Lyndsay C. Green. First published in *Detroit Free Press*, December 18, 2022. Copyright © 2022 by *Detroit Free Press*. Reprinted by permission of *Detroit Free Press*.

"The Elusive Roots of Rosin Potatoes" by Caroline Hatchett. First published in *The Bitter Southerner*, November 22, 2022. Copyright © 2022 by *The Bitter Southerner*. Reprinted by permission of *The Bitter Southerner*.

"Thanksgiving is an RPG" by Khadjiah Johnson. First published in *Black Nerd Problems*, November 25, 2022. Copyright © 2022 by *Black Nerd Problems*. Reprinted by permission of *Black Nerd Problems*.

"Restriction as Possibility; Lifestyle as Politics" by Alicia Kennedy. First published in *MOLD Magazine*, June 22, 2022. Copyright © 2022 by This is MOLD, Inc. Reprinted by permission of This is MOLD, Inc.

"The Double Life of New York's Black Oyster King" by Briona Lamback. First published in *Atlas Obscura*, September 28, 2022. Copyright © 2022 by Briona Lamback. Reprinted by permission of the author.

"There Is No Such Thing as Italian Food" by John Last. First published in *Noema*, December 13, 2022. Copyright © 2022 by John Last. Reprinted by permission of the author.

"Salt and Sex" by Amy Loeffler. First published in *Whetstone*, volume 10. Copyright © 2022 by Amy Loeffler. Reprinted by permission of the author.

"He Knew It All" by Hugh Merwin. First published in *Grub Street*, December 5, 2022. Copyright © 2022 by Vox Media, LLC. Reprinted by permission of Vox Media, LLC.

"What We Write About When We Write About Food" by Ligaya Mishan. First published in *T: The New York Times Style Magazine*, February 18, 2022. Copyright © 2022 by the New York Times Company. Reprinted by permission.

"Foraging New York City's Wild, Edible Margins with Journei Bimwala" by Grey Moran. First published in *Grist*, May 3, 2022. Copyright © 2022 by Grey Moran. Reprinted by permission of the author.

"Regulating the Food Industry: An Aspirational Agenda" by Marion Nestle. First published in *American Journal of Public Health*, May 25, 2022. Copyright © 2022 by American Journal of Public Health. Reprinted by permission.

"The FDA Is Coming for Your Almond Milk" by Tom Philpott. First published in *Mother Jones*, May 19, 2022. Copyright © 2022 by Foundation for National Progress. Reprinted by permission.

"Is the 'Future of Food' the Future We Want?" by Jaya Saxena. First published in *Eater*, January 5, 2022.Copyright © 2022 by Vox Media, LLC. Reprinted by permission of Vox Media, LLC.

"'You Don't Look Anorexic'" by Kate Siber. First published in *The New York Times Magazine*, October 18, 2022. Copyright © 2022 by Kate Siber. Reprinted by permission of the author.

"Teach a Man to Fish" by Kayla Stewart. First published in *Gravy*, Winter 2022. Copyright © 2022 by Kayla Stewart. Reprinted by permission of the author.

"Time Is Strong" by David Streitfeld. First published in *Slow Reader Magazine* Volume 2: M.F.K. FISHER. Copyright © 2022 by David Streitfeld. Reprinted by permission of the author.

"Border Lines" by Anya Von Bremzen. First published in *Afar*, August 16, 2022. Copyright © 2022 by Anya Von Bremzen. Reprinted by permission of the author.

"What Counts as Fresh Food?" by Bee Wilson. First published in the *Wall Street Journal*, May 14, 2022. Copyright © 2022 by Bee Wilson. Reprinted by permission of the author.

Contents

Contents

Foreword

FOR FIVE OR six years now, I have been reading and thinking about food writing, not as my primary job, but as a sort of side gig. For me, this has kept it manageable yet still enjoyable. I also like to think it has given me some sort of distance from the world of "food media," whatever that may be today. I think it keeps me somewhat honest, too: I am an avid reader of all things related to food, but mainly as a consumer and, I suppose, a semi-professional critic.

I'm both happy and sad to admit that that world I've tried to keep my distance from—the clubby world of people who work at the country's top food and wine magazines and newspapers, who all know each other from the same industry functions—barely exists anymore anyway. And even in the ways that it does, it's much smaller, much less consequential. That is both a shame and truly for the best.

At least a decade before this series came into being in 2018, the food media world was already in crisis: Condé Nast's flagship food magazine, *Gourmet*, was shuttered. Food blogs were some combination of startups, message boards, and passion projects. Today, that whole world has turned upside down: Very few of the glossy magazines and household names still exist, and many have gone all or mostly digital. Big, stalwart brands have made way for dozens of smaller, niche independent publications and outfits. The Davids have become the Goliaths to boot: When I first started work on this series, I would remind myself to try to look beyond the *New York Times* and *The New Yorker*; these days I always end up with too many entries from *Eater* on my spreadsheet.

For all that change in whatever the world of "food media" once was or now is, I can confidently say that the pages of this book are all the better for it. Change and adaptation have been good. Between being forced to look elsewhere and find new sources and a proliferation of smaller, more independently driven outlets, I've found my long lists and spreadsheets have actually grown with each year I work on the series. That is, of course, due in part to my knowing where to look, but it's also due to an expanding appetite.

That has been the sustaining challenge: always looking around corners, finding great writing in completely unexpected places, and being ever more flexible in the definition of what counts as writing about food. Once upon a time I might have told you that the pinnacle of food writing was a reported *New Yorker* essay about all the science and engineering that went into breeding the most perfectly juicy, crisp apple. Today I can confidently tell you there is so much more out there, and I see it everywhere I look. (This is obviously also a reflection of my own maturity and expanding palate as an editor over the years.)

I can also say there is simply no one definition, no paragon, no truest, most perfect form of food writing. This series has grown to include criticism, fiction, academic writing, and even newsletters. And beyond just writing about ingredients, meals, and recipes, the collections now include writing about all manner of topics relating to the world of food. Some of my favorites have been the more absurd: writing about fake plastic food, writing about food that jiggles, writing about food emojis that stand in for sexual symbols, and, of course, writing about what happens to our food *after* we eat it. But writing about food can also be difficult: writing about exploitative labor practices, writing about hunger and drought, writing about eating disorders.

Working on this series has made me a better, more flexible editor, a wider reader than I ever imagined. A true virtue of this process has also been having an open policy: Through reader and editor submissions sent via email, I get to read stories I never would have found on my own. Sure, it means inviting a lot of traffic into my inbox, but it undoubtedly has helped me find things I never would have known existed without tips from friends, acquaintances, and perfect strangers. For being such a lonely job—compiling a list and deciding what you think of it—it also has its very fun social moments. Asking people for help with submissions is, in my opinion, not just helpful, but in fact a crucial and necessary part of the process. I have learned from the best editors in the business to ask others for their input, their suggestions, and their insight, and to be gracious about admitting that no one person can consume it all.

I am so grateful to HarperCollins for the opportunity to work on this series as long as I have. I am thankful for my editor Jessica Vestuto's reliability and patience with me, and of course I must give all credit for my involvement with this series and its existence in the first place to Naomi Gibbs. Naomi is a brilliant editor with a true nose for talent. (I am not just saying that because she picked me; Naomi has edited *real* authors like Ursula K. Le Guin, Alexander Chee, and Nana Kwame Adjei-Brenyah.)

As of this writing, I will be handing over the series editor duties to Jaya Saxena, a writer and editor whose work has been featured in this volume several times over. For me, Jaya represents the present and future of food writing—and all that it is capable of doing and becoming. I am so thrilled for her and excited to see where she takes this volume next. You can send submissions for next year's edition to her at bestamericanfoodwriting@gmail.com. According to our guidelines, anything that was published in a North American periodical during the year 2023 is eligible for inclusion in the volume. If you have submitted in the past: Thank you so much, and please do so again.

Onward and upward with food writing!

SILVIA KILLINGSWORTH

Introduction

EVERYONE WITH UNLIMITED access to some kind of food—the majority of people in this country—takes it for granted. We live five minutes from a banana or a Slurpee or a cheeseburger and we consider that normal, even though everything it takes to bring us those things is part of a deeply flawed and destructive system.

On the other hand, a carrot in the ground out back, an egg from a local chick, represent life and love. As much as anything, food must be seen in context; it's a lens through which we can view just about everything humans do. Although it's one of the joys of our lives, it's also not a pretty picture when you stare right at it, like an alluring magic eye that resolves to an apocalypse.

There are no records, but it's safe to believe that chatting about food is about as old as verbal communication, and that food writing and food art are as old as writing and art. We are rightly obsessed with food, as were most of our ancestors; it's not only a true need, it's a fundamental source of pleasure.

And so it's an understatement to call food an important subject.

But because food writing is *so* broad and necessary, it's difficult to write about it generally. What is food writing? That definition has shifted with the judgment of writers (and, perhaps especially, with that of editors).

Even "food" is not a strictly defined word: The dictionary says that it's "any nutritious substance that people or animals eat or drink or that plants absorb in order to maintain life and growth." But there is "food" that doesn't provide nourishment and indeed makes us ill. (By dictionary definition, that should be called "poison.") And, these days, those who write about "food" produce work about all things related to food, everything from farming to indigestion. (An article in serious contention for inclusion in this collection, for example, is about shit.)

In the beginning, people mostly wrote about growing, irrigation, famines, water, feasts, gratitude for bountiful harvests and grief for meager ones—mostly guides for the living and entreaties to the divine—and farming and eating in general. There's a Sumerian document from 1500 BCE or so in which a father verbally walks his son through their farm, instructing him on planting, sowing, and reaping procedure.

The ancient Greek poet Hesiod was an early romancer of food: "Let me have a shady rock and wine of Biblis, a clot of curds and milk of drained goats with the flesh of a heifer fed in the woods, that has never calved, and of firstling kids; then also let me drink bright wine, sitting in the shade . . ." The great early international travelers, from the seventh-century Buddhist monk Xuanzang to Marco Polo, all reported on the foods they discovered and were often responsible for their spread—or their theft.

In almost any culture, at any time, you can find food writing, because food means growing and hardship, and health and medicine, and pleasure and craving, and work and holiday. Food is more than a necessity, it is a global obsession, something everyone thinks about every hour. In its abundance it is a gift and a joy, and in its absence a curse and a tragedy. If a culture has writing, that culture has food writing.

Bread riots are almost as old as bread and so hardly a new thing, but food and land and agriculture played an important role not only as catalysts of the revolutionary periods of the eighteenth and nineteenth centuries but in the writing about them. The best known of the food theorists of this era was probably Brillat-Savarin, who's been reduced to "You are what you eat." Longer legs can be attributed to Thomas Malthus, who observed that the ever-increasing yields of agriculture led to an ever-increasing number of mouths to feed, and that this was a system doomed to failure, a cycle that would spin toward global starvation and death. More than a century later, Paul Ehrlich made a similar argument in *The Population Bomb*.

In the nineteenth century, Karl Marx presciently noted that

without many restrictions or rules to feed an increasingly large and wealthy population, modern agriculture posed a uniquely novel kind of threat. He critiqued monoculture, row-cropping, and the application of imported fertilizers (the "new" style of farming) as "robbing" the soil, and lamented the end of "self-sustaining agriculture," describing a "system of exhaustion in North America," where "it was cheaper and more profitable to clear and crop new land than to renovate the old."

By now two distinct threads of food writing had emerged: one concerned with how we'd feed ourselves, and the other with how much we'd enjoy it. This second thread was primarily literary. The era's Western novelists, like Dickens and Austen and Balzac, spent pages writing about food, and much of that writing has a sound that would not be out of place in this collection. From *Great Expectations*: "My sister had a trenchant way of cutting our bread-and-butter for us that never varied. First, with her left hand she jammed the loaf hard and fast against her. Then she took some butter (not too much) on a knife and spread it on the loaf, in an apothecary kind of way, as if she were making a plaister—using both sides of the knife with a slapping dexterity, and trimming and moulding the butter off round the crust . . ." (It's a much longer description; Dickens, as you know, was paid by the word.)

Zola, the so-called father of naturalism, could and did write about peasants starving while the aristocracy feasted: "Du pain! du Pain! du Pain! cry the starving striking miners, while in the boss's home the cook anxiously awaits her order of 'croutes de vol-au-vent' . . ."

But he also was expert in writing about food as metaphor, in a style that was sometimes more than a little over-the-top: "[F]or the most part the cheeses stood in piles. . . . A gigantic *cantal* was spread on leaves of white beet, as though split by blows from an axe; then came . . . a *gruyere* like a wheel fallen from some barbarian chariot, some Dutch cheeses suggesting decapitated heads smeared in dried blood and as hard as skulls. . . ." Was Zola paid by the simile?

The miserable ways in which food was produced, like adulteration—milk augmented with plaster of paris, for example— or the filthy conditions and near-torture of workers (documented, of course, in *The Jungle*) were phenomena that brought solid journalists into writing about food, and eventually spawned federal regulation. But the growing concern among those who bothered with human welfare remained, "How do we make it so everyone eats well?"

The nineteenth century brought nutrition into the spotlight, where it's remained. Among the earliest notable American food writers was pioneering farmer and advisor George Washington Carver, whose still-in-print ode to the peanut (*How to Grow the Peanut: and 105 Ways of Preparing It for Human Consumption*) was at least a half-century ahead of its time in stating what has only recently become obvious: that legumes are and should be the most important source of protein for humans.

As the methods of growing food shifted in the ways Marx feared, popular but serious writing about food, agriculture, and their role in humanity's well-being began to fade in the first quarter of the twentieth century, as the main concerns changed from how to grow enough good food to how to grow more than enough food that could be traded at a profit. That would have made an interesting subject, but few seem to have tackled it directly.

The Europeans Rudolf Steiner, Albert Howard, and Lady Eve Balfour were advocates for sensible farming and eating but, aside from Carver, little was written in the American press about this subject until Frances Moore Lappé, responding to Malthus and her contemporary Ehrlich, produced the all-important *Diet for a Small Planet* in 1971, which argued that only by growing food to support a diet stressing legumes and whole grains could we hope to feed everyone well. (That was the most meaningful piece of food writing to come out of the twentieth century.)

Most mid-century writing about agriculture was technical, and that which wasn't fell squarely in the realm of home economists. Recipes were published in the food pages (or, more likely, "women's pages") of almost every newspaper in the country, along with some lame or at best inoffensive (and sometimes even helpful) copy. Women were being instructed, convinced, guided to learn to cook with the new "convenient" ingredients, many of which were unfamiliar until mid-century. Much of this would fall closer to the realm of marketing than that of literature.

But with World War Two came *Gourmet*, and other magazines about or including food followed soon thereafter; then there appeared more ambitious cookbooks (*Mastering the Art of French Cooking* was published in 1961). Newspapers sought to try to find that same readership, a mostly urban and suburban group that wanted to produce more interesting food than, let's say, chicken à la king, one that was even beginning to become interested in restaurants outside of the local Chinese or Italian, and even bold and wealthy enough to begin to travel, first to the culinary mecca of Paris but eventually to Italy and elsewhere.

Exploration, enjoyment, discerning taste, even hedonism were not new. In fact they all hearkened back to way before Brillat-Savarin, because the *Epic of Gilgamesh* (2000 BCE, more or less) instructs us to "Fill your belly. Day and night make merry. Let days be full of joy. Dance and make music day and night. . . . These things alone are the concern of men." But the consideration of these things was nearly the exclusive domain of the food writing of the late twentieth century. Serious discussions about how to protect and fairly distribute land, how to raise crops that promoted health, how to best feed people—not just from the perspective of flavor but from that of morality and justice and what came to be called sustainability—were either ignored or relegated to academic journals and agricultural publications. The heirs to *The Jungle* would wait until the nineties or even later.

Meanwhile, the "food pages," by whatever name they went under, were a place where no one wanted to go to be challenged about real-world issues. You might be challenged to produce a new dish, or challenged to find the money to eat at Le Cirque (or better still Tour d'Argent), or buy a pair of shoes just like those of your favorite chef, but with rare exceptions you were not going to be forced in those pages to consider where your food came from, what was in it, or how your ability to procure it might be more taken for granted than it was for others. Thus the breed of food writing that focused almost entirely on the joys of cooking, pleasures of eating, excitement of finding "new" foods, a romantic swell, became the norm.

It seems in retrospect that food writing's mission was to promote opulence, pleasure, and over-satiation, a celebration of abundance. Gradually, as travel became easier, as other cultures became more accessible, as money became looser and adventuresome writers more numerous, we began to see the chronicling and codification of "important" ingredients, of luxury, of "great" meals that grew greater and greater and greater. Eventually, we were compelled to read descriptions of twenty-course tasting menus comprising, at least in part, ingredients most of us could never lay our hands on.

(The public epitome of all of this, although it now seems almost quaint compared to reports of the styles of contemporary billionaires, was the June 1976 auction dinner won by Craig Claiborne and Pierre Franey, who, for a bid of $300, were able to command a meal at Chez Denis in Paris. Comprising more than thirty dishes accompanied by nine wines, the bill for the meal—paid by American Express—was $4,000.)

This irritating trend, though not entirely scorned, now feels ridiculous, and is widely seen as such. (Although the job here is not to criticize it in detail; that work is thankfully being done elsewhere.)

There is a growing movement to write more personally, not only about wonderful and elite "foodie" experiences but painful or otherwise meaningful ones as well, and although it's safe to say that memoirists have carved out a prominent niche on the bestseller lists, food memoirists (and it's in this group we must include Proust as a pioneer) have found a particularly important role.

This kind of introspection, when well handled (as it is in many of the pieces in this collection), no longer entirely relies on the white American seeking to discover the foods of "other" cultures—although we still have plenty of that—but is now flush with a productive cross-pollination, of people exploring their own cultures, their own diverse neighborhoods, their own relationships with food within and around their families, in their cities and states and regions, as well as digging even deeper into the hands-on cooking and, even more novel, food production of nearly everywhere in the world.

This last is of primary importance, because it brings us full circle to the discussion of food as a critical element to humans, and not just as a source of pleasure: Food is in crisis, and, again, although this introduction is not the place for detailing that, this collection features a substantial number of pieces from both expected and unexpected sources on topics related to that. It has come to the attention of everyone who has the time and energy to consider these things that the way we produce and process food, the ways in which we make it available, are—along with climate change—among the greatest threats to human survival. Malthus was both right and wrong: We *can* produce enough food for everyone to thrive, but if we get it wrong it may produce widespread depopulation after all.

This is not an entirely new situation but the knowledge of it has only recently become widespread and widely acknowledged; it is justifiably trending among food (and finally other) writers, and it's about time. It could have happened sooner, but for decades food writers were actively discouraged from thinking about food as anything other than pleasurable. Those late-twentieth-century food writers could produce all they wanted about continental luxury hotels and their restaurants, about authenticity in Mongolia, about potatoes in Peru, about the mysterious ways of Japan, about the availability of sea urchin by mail, or how a home cook could produce deer—or tofu!—jerky, and so on, but they were for the most part forbidden from treading on the fields of sustainability, environmental pollution (food writers decidedly did not cover Rachel Carson), the decline of nutrition, the horrors of processing or labor: Leave those more serious and less-enchanting and -delightful subjects to your colleagues in Business or Health or Agriculture.

If there are food sections and magazines and websites that remain devoted to pleasure, publications that decidedly avoid the admittedly often unpleasant subjects of almost everything that happens from planting a seed to bringing a hand or a fork or a spoon or a chopstick to our mouths, that's fine; those of us who have time for it need diversion. But just as in the last few decades it's become widely recognized that Hollywood and sports—which ostensibly exist for our entertainment—are giant businesses with often distasteful and reactionary and even destructive sides, it's finally acknowledged that food does not just magically appear at farmers markets and restaurants and supermarkets; neither is it all grown or raised by happy workers under beautiful conditions.

Thus food writers have written about subjects as diverse as the grading of meat in slaughterhouses, the meals eaten by sailors in submarines, the impact of CRISPR technology on seeds, the diets of prisoners, perennial rice, the link between the defeat of Reconstruction and the near-disappearance of Black farmers from our landscape, the relationship between agriculture and nutrition and climate change and justice and more.

Food is grown and raised and caught everywhere, under all kinds of circumstances. Knowing about those various kinds of operations is a part of being a responsible eater and, since we are all eaters, a responsible human. We cannot, or at least should not, take food for granted, but wonder about and consider the way in which it's produced. What does the land look like? Who owns it? Who farms it? How? What are working conditions like, for farmworkers of course, but also for slaughterhouse workers, truckers, processors, packers, stockers, cashiers, servers? What's for sale? How's it cooked? Who can afford it? These questions are endless, and they're no less intriguing—and certainly no less important—than how beautiful it is or how great it tastes or how closely one associates it with one's grandmother.

So. Here, then, is the gamut, from a full-blown and imaginative manifesto from Marion Nestle, the doyenne of food politics, to a meta-story about food writing from *New York Times* writer Ligaya Mishan; from a personal-is-political essay by Alicia Kennedy to Caroline Hatchett's magnificent dive into rosin potatoes, of which few of us have heard.

Like the authors, the publications are equally varied, from stalwarts like the *Times* and *Gastronomica* to worthy recent additions like *Civil Eats* and *Gastro Obscura*.

"Everything" is not here; a great variety of terrific food writing is, and it's with pride that we say that if it doesn't cover all the bases, it covers no superfluous ones. It's enough to make you take food seriously for a while, and to entertain you as well.

MARK BITTMAN

The Best
AMERICAN
FOOD
WRITING
2023

ALICIA KENNEDY

Restriction as Possibility;
Lifestyle as Politics

FROM *MOLD Magazine*

A FRIEND RECENTLY said to me that she is ok with lifestyle journalism making people uncomfortable. In light of how our world is raging with injustice, climatic and otherwise, I couldn't agree more. As a food writer, I think lifestyle media, so long siloed away from the dirty business of politics, needs to engage with the realities of the world.

Climate justice is a main concern for me, as I live in Puerto Rico, where the effects of 2017's category five Hurricane Maria still linger and every year a new hurricane season looms. There are plenty of reasons for lifestyle media to engage with the reality of racial, gender, and labor injustice that all intersect with climate change and have very real implications for how, especially, to eat.

Though it's become common to repeat the refrain that "100 companies are responsible for 71 percent of greenhouse gas emissions," the study from which that statistic emerged focused only on fossil fuels; and while incredibly significant, it's been watered down to suggest that there can be no worthwhile change on an individual scale or in other sectors. With food, our consumption patterns are inextricably tied with larger environmental and labor considerations. Currently, the global food system accounts for nearly a third of greenhouse gas emissions, and land use for livestock production has been a devastating force of deforestation, using up 80 percent of global farmland to provide fewer than 20 percent of the calories consumed globally. As of 2020, the food system of the

United States accounted for 19.7 million full- and part-time jobs. Meatpacking companies lied at the beginning of the COVID-19 pandemic about a meat shortage in order to force people back to work without the proper protective conditions, leading to 269 deaths. Earlier this year, fast food and farmworkers marched in Florida for better conditions. The federal minimum wage in the U.S. has stayed stagnant at $7.25 per hour despite intense inflation.

As our day-to-day lives become so encumbered by expensive necessities, housing insecurity, and looming natural disasters, the question I consistently ask is: Where is lifestyle media? It's pondering whether burger rankings are still important; it's accepting defeat and painting a picture of the future of food that relies on lab meat fantasies. Changing diets, though, is a crucial climate change mitigation strategy. This means changing our lifestyles: how we live them, of course, but also how we write about them and how we share them.

Recipes, in particular, could be written in ways that push people toward different understandings of access, regionalism, and seasonality. They can force a reckoning between the false universality of the American supermarket and one's actual regional food system. But that's only if they're written in a way that challenges dependence upon the animal products and imported products that are known to be ecologically destructive. Rather than think of this as a restriction, it can open up possibilities for variations.

Consumption as we know it, based on the endless growth that capitalism demands, attempts to abolish alternate possibilities for regionalism and new ways of living. While the crisis of climate change has undoubtedly been caused by fossil fuel companies, it is also the responsibility of those living especially in the United States and other rich nations to change our lifestyles to fit in with the environment's clear demands for us to tread more lightly. And it's ever more important for those who have economic ability and cultural capital to model behaviors that make treading lightly seem easy and desirable, to show that what has been proffered as "restriction" actually houses the possibility for pleasure and connection, as well as a foundation for bigger change.

Chafing at the idea of personal responsibility here is understandable, but lifestyle choices have ripple effects. A fast fashion dress purchase might seem like a reasonable way to dress nicely, cheaply, yet the person who sewed it across the globe is poorly paid and treated, and most of the overproduction of these companies ends up polluting other poorer nations. Demand for one kind of banana, a convenient and cheap supermarket snack, pollutes growing nations and pesticides poison farmworkers. One person in the United States' easy pleasures are another person's and ecosystem's burden.

This is what writers Markus Wissen and Ulrich Brand have called "the imperial mode of living." Their book of the same name breaks down "how normality is produced precisely by masking the destruction in which it is rooted," and this sense of normality experienced by people in the Global North as well as increasingly in some economically powerful nations understood as part of the Global South, is imperialist in nature. Climate change is one crisis that is encroaching upon that sense of normality, and continuing to live in an unchanged manner dependent on cheap goods made elsewhere and fossil fuel consumption seems to be more and more nihilist in nature. When does a cheap dress or cheap food become worth more than the continued existence of the planet? When will normality shift to encompass the well-being of everyone? These are questions of lifestyle, cultural norms, and collective change, which also need to become questions of lifestyle media.

In the United Nations IPCC's most recent climate change mitigation report, the word "lifestyle" appears 193 times. The authors write, "The acceptability of collective social change over a longer term towards less resource intensive lifestyles, however, depends on the social mandate for change. This mandate can be built through public participation, discussion and debate, to produce recommendations that inform policymaking."

When we say that changes only have to occur on the level of big policy and systems, we leave out the significance of public participation and the fact that how we each live our lives is part of a greater whole. While that would be fantastic, it feels more and more impossible without "collective social change"; these changes can occur through shifting norms and habits that will thus influence broader policy. "Shifts in development pathways result from both sustained political interventions and bottom-up changes in public opinion," the report says. "Collective action by individuals as part of social movements or lifestyle changes underpins system change." People decided to bring their own reusable bags to supermarkets, for example, and now states and municipalities have instituted single-use plastic bag bans.

When it comes to food consumption, an important aspect of changing lifestyle is increasing the desirability of plant-based diets specifically. This requires normalization, and perhaps a bit of discomfort. In what we call "lifestyle media," causing discomfort has always been a big no-no—opening up a food magazine to find anything about habit-changing for climate change might happen once per year, while steaks are on offer the other eleven months. Even vegetarian recipes are promoted in a special section, while lamb and chicken are the norm for the main.

How we live our lives, how we choose to move around the world and consume, has effects: Maybe we just feel slightly better, maybe we influence change in our immediate communities, maybe that change in our communities causes local policy change and eventual regulation of deeply destructive industries. The imperial mode in which people in the Global North consume will change, whether because of climate change and extreme weather events or as a way to stop it. Finding a way to create joy and collective participation in new modes of living is a political responsibility, and it offers new possibilities for our lives.

AMY LOEFFLER

Salt and Sex

FROM *Whetstone Magazine*

SACCHARINE CONFECTIONS ARE often associated with emotional love. From finely engraved chocolate Easter bunnies and crème-filled eggs to jellybeans and marshmallow Peeps, all classes of extravagant and inexpensive forms of sweets related to the vernal equinox are pregnant with procreative metaphor, rejuvenation, and endearment.

But to taste love itself, in the carnal sense, is most definitely a savory endeavor.

Even sugar enthusiasts such as anthropologist Dr. Sidney W. Mintz—whose extensive research focuses on the socioeconomic power structures spawned by delicate white sugar crystals—concede this point.

"If there were one taste one might expect to be linked with physical love, I suspect that it would not be the taste of sweet but the taste of salt," he wrote in the journal *MLN*.

Sweat, tears, and other delightfully messy secretions of romance and lovemaking certainly smack of the saline, a fact that has been acknowledged by humans for hundreds if not thousands of years. Culturally, scientifically, and historically, the more accurate symbol of our procreative nature is salt.

A disciple of Sigmund Freud's, Dr. Ernest Jones, who founded the London Psychoanalytical Society in October of 1913, espoused that many words related to an increase in desire have their roots in salt. For example, the term "salacious," meaning libidinous or lecherous, is derived from the Latin "salax."

Indeed, hopeful French housewives who lived on the cusp of the tail end of the Middle Ages would be befuddled by the modern-day hypervigilant warnings that caution salt restriction today. Sodium chloride was widely used by medieval ladies of the house to instill heat and spice in the marriage bed by quite literally sprinkling salt on their husbands.

As preposterous as sprinkling salt over a sexual partner is to modern sensibilities—as if prepping a chicken for roasting— medieval women were merely following the medical advice of the time. Advanced medical knowledge of the era was based upon the belief that salt was a stimulant akin to a saline version of Viagra.

Pop culture reinforced the notion of salt as a key to unlocking libidinous desires, most notably by numerous references in Shakespeare's plays acknowledging salt as a key ingredient to heightened sexual arousal.

In *The Merry Wives of Windsor*, Shakespeare's tale of love and mischief in a suitor's attempt to woo two wealthy women, the exchange between Master Page and Master Shallow draws a correlation between salt and a youthful libido:

> Though we are justices and doctors and churchmen, Master
> Page, we have some salt of our youth in us; we are the sons of
> women, Master Page.

In *Othello*, when antagonist Iago tries to convince Othello how difficult it is to get proof of Desdemona cheating with Cassio, he invokes salt to represent unbridled passion.

> It is impossible you should see this,
> Were they as prime as goats, as hot as monkeys,
> As salt as wolves in pride, and fools as gross
> As ignorance made drunk.

Salt as Myth
Salt has historically been so imbued with the power to evoke desire that it became synonymous with carnal love.

Jones is referenced by German ethnologist Leo Frobenius in his discovery of an African folktale that describes a journey in which the characters Penis and Vagina serve as anthropomorphized protagonists and must protect the salt they are carrying from dissolving in the rain.

The enduring folktale is thought to have come into Frobenius' purview from his numerous trips to Africa, where he interacted with populations in central Nigeria among others. It is just one of many tales that cemented, according to Frobenius, the salty nature of sex and love and why the penis is ever seeking of the "daintiest delicacy [salt] while the vagina always wants more salt [the salty semen from the penis]," as quoted in the untitled piece of folk wisdom.

Greek historian, biographer, and essayist Plutarch promoted the libidinous properties of salt in various essays and musings about quotidian life in the Panhellenic world. He cites examples of celibate Egyptian priests who were known to abstain from the delicate white flakes of sodium chloride at certain times of the year as it was thought to increase libido. The scholar also wrote that dogs that had failed to reproduce could be given salt and some fresh meat to aid in copulation and reproduction.

Love Is in the (Salt) Air

One of the more prominent symbols of salt and its generative powers of procreation is Aphrodite, the Greek goddess of love, beauty, and fertility. Her origin story occurs in the saltwater that surrounds Cyprus. According to Greek legend, she was born from sea foam that was inoculated with sperm from her father Uranus' split genitals.

Aphrodite's birth was popularized in the work *Theogony* by the poet Hesiod. Hers is a tale of outrageous filial betrayal of Uranus, who is castrated by his own son, causing the remnants of his mutilated scrotum to birth Aphrodite in the froth of the Cypriot sea:

"And white foam spread around them from the immortal flesh, and in it grew a maiden . . . and came forth an awful and lovely goddess . . . Gods and men call her Aphrodite and Aphrogenia (the foam-born) because she grew amid the foam."

Indeed, from her name comes the word "aphrine," referring to the nascent delicate white crystals that develop when saltwater begins to evaporate and negative chlorine ions coalesce with positively charged sodium ions to form sodium chloride.

Aphrodite's association with sex was manifested in the ancient world by the formation of a cult devoted to her that exalted femininity and practiced ritual sex work. Under the auspices of Aphrodite that custom began in 1500 BCE and flourished throughout Greece.

Earlier iterations of the goddess known as Ishtar in Assyria were also known to have practiced ritual sex and this may be where the custom originated. Gatherings of the cult of Aphrodite were thought to be widespread during festivals held in the goddess's honor, which mandated that young maidens make a pilgrimage to her temples, where they were obliged to have sex with strangers. Members of her cult carried pouches of salt denoting their devotion to her.

The rituals solidified the connection between sex and salt, and the myth of Aphrodite herself also codified the notion in popular culture that salt had generative powers. Plutarch's musings of after-dinner chats, *Symposiakon* (*Table Talk*), promoted this idea and reflected in his collection that salt was not only an impetus for copulation but an actual ingredient for procreation, noting that "the ships that carry salt breed a profusion of mice."

This notion was also supported in Greek philosopher Aristotle's *History of Animals*: "Some people say, indeed stoutly maintain that, if they merely lick salt, mice become pregnant."

Mammals, Moths, and Making Love
The myth of Aphrodite added an easily digestible populist narrative to a belief that salt was an intrinsically beneficial mineral to enhance reproductive processes. Aristotle took a keen interest in salt's association with reproduction as well, though he didn't care much for the mythology of the gods.

Specifically, he noticed that sheep fared well when given salt in their regular diets by shepherds. He promoted the virtues of the mineral as part of his interest in the environment and health, observing, "that sheep are in a better condition by keeping their hydro-mineral balance in check, and that animals that drink saline water can copulate earlier. Salt must be given to them before they give birth and during lactation."

Modern science has since discovered the positive effect of an infusion of salt on the nervous system, and for lactating mammals, but a tiny male moth with a huge appetite for salt also seems to back the notions of the ancient Greeks—that salt is a key ingredient for successful sex.

The male Gluphisia moth spends most of his short life accumulating enough salt to give his mate a nuptial gift of sodium.

This act is achieved by "puddling," or sucking from pools of standing water or moist ground for several hours at a time and squirting out the liquid in strong jets. The process is nothing if not a test of endurance, with the most virile moths squirting out 4,325 jets, or 600 times their bodyweight.

The moth only takes in sodium, expelling other nutrients like potassium. The act raises the moth's sodium levels to eight times that of the nonpuddling Gluphisia. Ultimately, the former will give half of this sodium to a mate in a reproductive act by incorporating the sodium into spermatophore, a present of nutrients, protein, and sperm that supplies the female with enough sodium to pass on to her larvae.

While mammals don't exhibit the puddling behavior, a German idiom makes note of cooks in love adding too much salt to the soup, which certainly speaks to the abundance of salt required to maintain the state of being in love and its associated activities.

And it seems humans really do require more salt when the love bug bites.

In 2013, the Technology Transfer Center (TTZ) in Bremerhaven, Germany, conducted a study about hormones and their relationship to taste. The study yielded intriguing information about humans in love and their ability to detect certain categories of taste like bitter, sweet, salty, and umami. Researchers found that couples who had recently fallen in love had a much higher tolerance for salt, as compared to single people and those in long-term relationships who fared better in detecting the nuances of taste.

When we fall in love, hormones are released that affect many biological markers, including dopamine. Sexual attraction relates to the dopaminergic reward system, and salt is intricately involved in the regulation of that system as well as is important for motor functions and general arousal. Some researchers believe it may have some relationship to the mechanics of ejaculation and neuroendocrine consequences of sexual activity, or to other processes pertaining to lovemaking.

Like moths, humans appear to require more salt when amorous feelings are at their peak.

Culturally, historically, and physically, the taste of love is firmly entrenched in the saline. Indeed, salt is necessary for most, if not all, of the body's physiological processes. Mintz recounts that we don't nutritionally require sucrose in forms like corn syrup or cane sugar, thanks to the body interpreting almost all foods besides animal flesh as a form of glucose. But our bodies require sodium chloride to perform all of our physiological tasks, including generating the delightful corporeal elixir for sex and love.

What's love got to do with salt? Pretty much everything.

Border Lines

FROM *Afar*

IT'S 11 A.M. in Gaziantep, a city in southeastern Türkiye, and I'm stunned by the sheer spectacle of our late breakfast. My partner, Barry, and I are at a restaurant called Orkide with our friend Filiz Hösükoğlu, an expert in local culture and food. Around us, guys in trim leather jackets and ladies—some in sparkly black tops, some in flowing hijabs—sip menengiç, a warm drink made from ground wild pistachios.

I circle our table in awe, trying to count and record all the dishes, losing track at three dozen. There are snowy clumps of *kaymak* (clotted buffalo cream) to be eaten with raw honey from the nearby hills; eggs scrambled with walnuts, fresh tarragon, and tiny roasted green olives; and eggs fried with topaç (beef confit). Copper bowls hold apricots stewed with fresh almonds and tahini the color of deep earth. All dishes seem touched by mint, live fire, and flakes of local red pepper.

"This spread is my homage to our region's Sunday tradition of potluck family breakfasts," says Mustafa Özgugüler, Orkide's owner, as a vast platter of *katmer* arrives. A delicate cousin of the city's prodigious baklava, katmer is made by wrapping layers of paper-thin pastry around pulverized pistachios with an almost preternatural intensity, and then baking it all to a sugary crunch. "Katmer is a cult, a drug . . ." Filiz murmurs.

I'd been dreaming about Gaziantep—Türkiye's sixth-largest city, situated just west of the Euphrates River and north of the Syrian border, since I discovered its flavors in Istanbul two decades ago at

Çiya, a celebrated restaurant specializing in southeastern Turkish cuisine. The food at Çiya was vibrant and inventive, wild with fresh herbs, pomegranate molasses, and şalça (sun-dried tomato and pepper pastes). It seemed worlds away from the delicate refinement of Istanbul cooking, and it launched in me a mild obsession with Gaziantep. Still, for years I hesitated to go, always too busy in Istanbul, and anxious perhaps that reality might not live up to my expectations. Meanwhile, the food hype only grew, especially when UNESCO named Gaziantep a Creative City of Gastronomy in 2015.

While I'd been putting off a visit, geopolitics in this region kept on its dark course. In 2011, Syrian president Bashar al-Assad's regime began to use violence to suppress pro-democracy protests—tactics that eventually launched a ruinous civil war in Syria. During the next decade, that conflict would send more than 3.5 million refugees across the border to Türkiye. Megalopolis Istanbul absorbed some 550,000 arrivals. Gaziantep welcomed at least 500,000, ballooning its population by almost a third—and earning its mayor, Fatma Şahin, international praise for her savvy policies that prioritized integration and tolerance.

For the past several years, I've been researching a new book on food and nationalism, and soon after wrapping the text, I decided it was finally time for a visit. Like all food-obsessed pilgrims to Antep, as the locals call Gaziantep, I'd come for kebabs of grass-fed lamb, *lahmacun* (flatbreads with toppings) blistered in wood-fired ovens, and tiny bulgur dumplings bobbing in yogurt soup. Less blithely, I hoped to break bread with Syrians making a go of it. I wanted to learn how the new arrivals—most from war-ravaged Aleppo, once Syria's largest city, 61 miles south—are reshaping the food culture of this singular borderland. From my book research, I was already familiar with Istanbul's post-imperial Balkan Greek Armenian assemblage. Now I wanted to know more about what had been happening in Gaziantep—once a critical trading hub along the Silk Road—with its intertwined, ever-shifting layers of cuisines, identities, and cultural memories.

"Of course, a hundred years ago there was no Türkiye or Syria." This reminder comes from Cevdet and Murat Güllü, owners of Elmaci Pazari Güllüoğlu, a legendary baklava shop in Antep's historic bazaar quarter, and the second stop on my first day in town, with Filiz showing the way. Along with their pistachio confections, glistening with syrup and sheep's butter, the brothers—whose great-grandfather founded the shop—offer historical context. They share that this region was once the Ottoman province of Haleb. Aleppo was the center of cuisine, culture, and commerce, and Antep was a provincial subdistrict.

In the mid-19th century, the Güllüs' great-grandfather, Çelebi, stopped in Aleppo on his religious hajj from Antep to Mecca. Awed by the city's baklava, he returned after his hajj to learn about the business, eventually moving back to Antep. In 1871, he started the shop that still exists today. By the time the Ottoman Empire officially dissolved in 1922—more than 70 years after the Güllüs' great-grandfather apprenticed in Aleppo—war and politics had drastically rearranged borders, official identities, and historical destinies. Colonial powers carved up the Levant (now Israel, Palestine, Jordan, Lebanon, and Syria) into British and French spheres of influence, while Mustafa Kemal Atatürk—"Father Turk"—forged the modern republic of Türkiye. (The independent republic of Syria didn't emerge until 1944.)

Almost instinctively, we tend to assign national identities to dishes, forgetting that borders are fluid, that so many of the boundaries we think of as fixed are both contorted and recent. And so, my mouth full of baklava, I ask the brothers, "Can one even say that baklava is Turkish or Syrian?" *Well* . . . they reply. It's *complicated.* Because after Türkiye's founding, Antep's *baklavaci* (baklava makers) did develop a style of their own: stretching the pastry so thin you can almost see through it, then dusting the pastry with starch to make it more delicate, pouring hot syrup over hot baklava after its time in a wood-fired oven. The resulting confection is very different from the Aleppo original, which has thicker pastry and is drier and less sweet. Today, Filiz adds, Antep is legendary as Türkiye's baklava capital, supplying 95 percent of what's sold in the country.

Leaving the brothers, Filiz leads us on a quick tour of the Coppersmith Bazaar's vaulted lanes, which resound with the tuk-tuk-tuk of artisans stamping their wares. I feel lucky to have her as our guide. In addition to being a walking encyclopedia of local food mores, she's an experienced NGO hand who specializes in integrating migrants through programs including vocational training. That night, for an introduction to the Syrian perspective on culinary and cultural matters, she arranges a dinner with her friend Yakzan Shishakly. We're to meet at Hişvahan, a restaurant in a 16th-century caravansary (guesthouse) that's been converted into a chic little hotel. When we arrive, Yakzan is already there, nursing a raki, Türkiye's anise-flavored alcohol, at a candlelit table. "The food here's outstanding," he says. "Plus, it's one of the few places in town serving drinks." He looks like he needs one.

In his early forties, Yakzan evokes an empathetic bon vivant who has taken on a tragic, impossible job. A grandson of Adib Shishakli—one of Syria's first presidents, who was assassinated in 1964—he grew up in Damascus. In 1999, he emigrated to Houston, became a U.S. citizen, and ran a successful air-conditioning business. Then, in 2011, "Syria happened," as he puts it.

Heartsick and desperate to help, Yakzan soon found himself back in Syria, where he witnessed hundreds of internally displaced persons (IDPs) surviving in flimsy tents beneath olive trees. He started raising funds to build a camp just north of Idlib, 41 miles from Aleppo. By mid-2012, Yakzan's Olive Tree, the first major displaced-persons camp in Syria, was a vast tent city of more than 20,000 IDPs. (Today, there are more than 180,000 IDPs in the camp.) Currently, his NGO, the Maram Foundation, manages five camps and gives logistical support to more than a dozen others. Although he can no longer travel freely in Syria for fear of kidnapping or assassination, from his office in Antep Yakzan addresses endless crises—to say nothing of the hopelessness of a war without end, a generation of kids in camps with no schools. How does he cope? A resigned little grin: "I listen to motivational speeches first thing each morning."

Yet Yakzan doesn't want to spend our dinner stereotyping Syrians as abject hands outstretched for NGO aid. This, he says, deprives them of dignity. The reality outside camps is of a normal lived life, especially in places such as Antep, which has absorbed a wide swath of Aleppo's middle class. Though, he adds, the trauma is always close to the surface: sudden tears for no reason, a fight with a taxi driver.

"Is it a comfort that the culture and food are so similar?" I ask, remembering suddenly the piercing alienation I experienced tasting American dishes back in the 1970s, soon after my mother and I arrived in the United States as refugees from the USSR.

"Of course, it softens the culture shock," Yakzan agrees as a waiter delivers spicy dips and stuffed vegetables. "There's our shared love of pomegranates, hot peppers, and olives, our pistachio fixation." A serious cook himself ("It helps with the stress"), Yakzan takes an appraising bite of eggplant-and-tomato dolmas. "[The dolmas] are the same concept as ours but with different spicing," he pronounces. Ditto the *içli köfte*, fried torpedo-shaped bulgur shells with a meaty, oniony filling—*kibbeh* to Syrians—of which Aleppo has many more varieties. "Then again," he emphasizes, "Syrian food varies hugely from Damascus to Homs to Aleppo."

I recall the words of Armenian writer Takuhi Tovmasyan: "Cuisines don't have nationalities, only geographies." And so, I ask the question that's been on my mind: Are Syrians here reshaping local food and restaurant culture? "Ah, journalists," Yakzan laughs in response, "always looking for catchy headlines!"

Integration is happening, he says. The city has built houses for refugees within neighborhoods, rather than setting them up in camps on the perimeter. It ensured that all city resources were available to locals and newcomers alike, including community centers where classes in cooking and dancing were offered in both Turkish and Arabic. But integration can be subtle and slow, Yakzan admits—even in this city promoted as a model of tolerance.

"In any society, foreigners are seen as a threat," he continues. Locals were curious about Syrian flatbread, though hesitant to act on their curiosity; they'd buy the bread in secret at night. "But now it's a part of the culture, plus countless other small interchanges," Yakzan says. "A Syrian cook uses local mint in a dish instead of Aleppo's cilantro. A Syrian restaurant puts a Turkish dish on the menu. A Turk buys our seven-spice mix from a Syrian grocer."

I think about Yakzan's reflections on the melding of cultures the following morning while sampling *lokum* (Turkish delight). I meet with confectioner and business owner Emel Shamma in the fluorescent brightness of Antep's Women Entrepreneur Support Center. Born and raised in Aleppo, she arrived in Antep in 2017 after four months in a refugee camp, where she witnessed phosphorus bombs exploding from planes, among other horrors. At the time, she was a struggling young mom with just a few gold bracelets to

her name. Then she saw the local Chamber of Industry's ad for
vocational training and began apprenticing at an Antep lokum
factory. A U.N. grant enabled her to launch her own business
two years ago. Now she's a poster child of Syrian female success
in Gaziantep, making a full ton of lokum a day and exporting to
several countries in Europe and beyond.

By habit, we associate lokum—from the Arabic *rahat-ul-hulkum*—
with Türkiye. But these jewel-like candies were also a huge part of
life back in Aleppo, given as gifts to celebrate the birth of a child
or a pilgrim's return from hajj. Finding Turkish lokum flavors a
bit alien, Emel began developing her own, creating unique spice
mixes with mastic (a piney resin), muscat, and cardamon. She
splurged on aromatic dried Isparta roses and ensured the pistachios were freshly cracked to retain their intensity, a trick she'd
learned from her family, who owned pistachio groves in Aleppo.

"I think of lokum as an amber," she says, "blending tastes of
home with those of my new country." Sampling a red, pomegranate-
flavored "amber" with emerald pistachios suspended in it—unlike
any lokum I've had in Türkiye—I reflect that this is the kind of cultural "fusion" Yakzan spoke of. It's not an easily digestible headline,
but a small, subtle detail—a tweak. One that might incrementally
accumulate, with other tweaks, into a changed food identity for
the city. Emel agrees. "Antep and Aleppo are like twins raised in
two countries," she muses. "Separated by war but brought together
again."

As I wander later that day, echoes of Aleppo seem to be everywhere, if one looks.

They're in the Ottoman mosques and hammams built with
striped stone, constructed by order of Aleppo's governors in the
16th century. They're in the hilltop citadel (a smaller version of
the one that still stands in the Syrian city), and in the shiny cotton-
and-silk *kutnu* fabric, an important Aleppian craft item that, like
baklava, developed its own life in the Turkish Republic.

Eager for a taste of Aleppo cooking in Gaziantep, I'm excited when
Filiz arranges a lunch the next day at Lazord. This beloved Syrian
hangout exists in a modest strip of small businesses with perky
signage in Arabic and Turkish. Two others join us: Rami Sharrack,
a consultant on entrepreneurial projects for refugees, and a social
activist named Shukran, who fled Aleppo in 2013.

We chat as we swipe floppy Syrian bread into exceptional hummus and *mtebbel*, a creamy compound of eggplant and yogurt ("looser, tangier, with more olive oil than Turkish dips," Filiz assesses). Shukran—a gracious, middle-aged mother of nine adult children scattered across the world—recounts that, soon after landing in Antep, she founded a social initiative to support Syrian war widows through cooking. Starting with $1,000, Shukran rented and restored an abandoned house that now hosts 50 women at a time. "For them it's a safe house and an income," she says. It's also a chance to provide homesick members of the diaspora with such Syrian dishes as *makdous* (pickled stuffed eggplants) and *shish barak*, meat-filled dumplings in a garlic-yogurt sauce. And what does she miss? I ask. "Here, it's the same region, similar dishes," she says with a shrug. "Maybe wild summer herbs from our hills? Or the stew of the leafy plant we call *molokhia*?"

Rami chimes in: "Syrian farmers started growing molokhia in Türkiye and now export to other countries with large populations of Syrians. *And* Syrians here sell around 200,000 bags of *khubz* [bread] each morning," he adds. "All small but important success stories!"

While we talk, Lazord's owner, Lobna Helli, bustles around with her teenage daughter and her mother, prepping to distribute 100 meals for the poor, both Turkish and Syrian. They do this every Friday. Once an HR manager in Aleppo, Lobna fled to Antep in 2015 after her husband was imprisoned and tortured by the Assad regime. A modest loan from family enabled her to open a humble café. After COVID hit, she expanded with a charity kitchen called Humanity Gathers Us. She, like Shukran, wanted to connect Syrian women who cook from their homes. Now, she helps them market and sell their food, and funds and distributes grocery cards for the needy.

At a table draped with her grandmother's lace tablecloth—a memento of her past in Aleppo—Lobna catches her breath and joins us for her mother's fresh-baked *fatayer*, pies bulging with spinach. There's also *mumbar*, the dish all Syrians are homesick for, she says. She's stuffed the plump sausages with rice, chickpeas, meat, and her own special spice mix, intense with black pepper. Shukran is over the moon about the *yalanji*, grape leaves with a rice filling that almost throbs with red pepper and pomegranate. And what's the super-secret Aleppian touch that so strikingly sets it apart from the Turkish version? "*Ground coffee*," Shukran whispers. Louder, with an air of authority, she declares that 60 percent of dishes between Antep and Aleppo are similar. "But our Aleppo cuisine is more varied, adaptable, stretchable," she contends, as Filiz nods and smiles, diplomatically—and then can't help adding, "But only Antep has [the pastry] katmer!"

Soon, our stomachs are full, the plates cleared. Time seems to dissolve as I sit sipping syrupy-sweet Turkish (Arabic? Levantine?) coffee with these strong generous women, these community power-houses, as they sweetly parse variations in recipes and identities. At moments like this, it's hard not to fall for that enduring cliché of food as an existential comfort that ultimately helps bring us together. Even as, a few hundred miles away, across a border that didn't exist until the 20th century and remained porous until a brutal war severed these people from their homes, the conflict grinds on.

BEE WILSON

What Counts as Fresh Food?

FROM *The Wall Street Journal*

TO CELEBRATE THE spring in Rome, they sometimes eat a vegetable stew called vignarola. Like the summer succotash of the American South or the ratatouille of France, vignarola is a vegetable stew that, in its ideal form, is radiant with freshness. It is made from artichokes, tiny fresh fava beans, and freshly shelled peas, all braised together with spring onions and white wine with fresh mint added at the end. Vignarola is a mellow mixture of all things green and new. It would once have marked the start of the new season after the hungry gap of late winter. But in an era when frozen peas are available all year round, the dish's dazzling spring freshness no longer means as much.

The great miracle of our modern food system has been to supply us with the freshness of spring all year round—or at least with an approximation of it. We can buy juicy fragrant herbs in the depths of winter and spring chickens in the fall. When I find myself getting twinges of nostalgia for the food of the past, I remember how grim it must have been to survive for half the year on little but salt pork, bread, and molasses (as described in Laura Ingalls Wilder's books for children). Before refrigeration and modern methods of agriculture, even butter and eggs were seasonal foods. Nineteenth-century American cookbooks included unappetizing recipes for keeping eggs "perfectly good" by coating them in a thick layer of grease or submerging them in saltwater. Somehow, these don't sound perfectly good—or at least not as good as living in a time when fresh eggs are available year round.

On the other hand, in our world of apparent freshness, how

often do you ever taste something that is truly fresh? When you look closely, much supermarket produce isn't quite as fresh as it seems. I recently met a British farmer who produces salad greens. He told me that he can taste a huge difference between a leaf that is a day old and three days old and that by five days, the flavor is greatly dulled, but the leaves would still look green and bright, so the average shopper would be none the wiser. The same goes for much of the food you buy. The label says "fresh" but what this actually means is something closer to "not rotten."

Our entire food supply is based on the idea of "fresh" and "keeping things fresh." But to keep things fresh is a kind of contradiction or deception, because something can only be truly fresh when it is right out of the ground or just cooked. The "fresh" food and drink in our supermarkets has often been on a surprisingly long journey in the global cold chain before it reaches us. A case in point is "fresh" orange juice. According to the 2010 book *Squeezed: What You Don't Know About Orange Juice*, by Alissa Hamilton, "fresh" orange juice advertised as "not-from-concentrate" may sit for as long as a year in cold storage tanks before it is packaged and shipped to stores. This isn't at all the same thing as taking a whole orange, cutting it in half, and squeezing its bright juice straight into a glass as the perfume of the zest fills the air.

The word "fresh" is strangely hard to define, which was one of the themes of an excellent book from 2009 called *Fresh: A Perishable History*, by Susanne Freiberg. As consumers, we are constantly asking ourselves whether things are fresh enough. We sniff the bottle of milk before we pour it on our cereal; we inspect a fillet of fish with suspicious eyes before we buy it. But Ms. Freiberg notes that U.S. food law is fuzzier on the question of freshness than you might expect. Many refrigerated foods can be labeled as "fresh" even if they are weeks old, and fruit can still be "fresh" after it is irradiated or waxed. In 2000, the Food and Drug Administration held a meeting in Chicago to discuss the meaning of the term "fresh" and to decide whether there should be a more honest term to describe certain "fresh" foods that are actually processed. Should these be renamed "fresh-like"? A Florida lobbyist for the American Fresh Juice Council argued that it was pointless to try to pin the term down. "Fresh is not a measurement," he argued. "Fresh is a state of being."

I sometimes wonder whether the desire for freshness is, paradoxically, part of the appeal of processed food, with its many kinds of packaging for the purpose of sealing in and opening up. The crackle of a newly opened bag of chips, the fizz when you release the tab of a soda, the big reveal of peeling back the foil on a tub of sugary yogurt—all of these can feel like a fresh start, even if what's inside the packet isn't exactly fresh.

It may be impossible to measure true freshness in food, but you know it when you taste it. It is the sweet snap of a green bean that has been picked that day or the way a walnut tastes at the start of the season straight from the shell. A couple of years ago in the early summer, a friend served me a simple dish of boiled potatoes that were so fresh and waxy that every other potato I'd ever eaten seemed stale in my memory. It was similar to the moment I tasted freshly made sushi for the first time: I had no idea that the grains of rice could have such an ambrosial warm texture, sticky and separate at the same time.

Not every food needs to be fresh to be good. Vignarola aside, it is hard to beat a frozen pea. I also love pickled lemons and canned tomatoes and stinky aged cheeses. A canned peach is an under-rated thing, and a dried apricot is often tastier than a fresh one.

But there are certain rare times when you taste something so fresh it stops you in your tracks. For me, the food most likely to do this is asparagus, which is one vegetable I try to buy in bundles from the market ever since reading that the green spears start to lose their sugars even a day after harvest. Slightly less fresh aspar-agus is still a treat, of course. But there is something about a really fresh spear, trimmed of its tough stalk and simply steamed or roasted and dipped in hollandaise sauce, that tastes as fresh as sap rising. It is as if you are eating spring itself.

BRIONA LAMBACK

The Double Life of New York's Black Oyster King

FROM *Gastro Obscura*

IN THE HEART of New York's financial center, a vacant building has sat untouched for decades. Behind its unassuming brass shell is the story of New York City's once-famed oyster houses and the overlooked life of Thomas Downing, the city's Black oyster king.

During the 1800s, the elite flocked to Downing's Broad Street oyster house for a slurp of his freshest catch—considered the best in the city. Downing, born to formerly enslaved parents, rubbed elbows with wealthy aristocrats and businessmen throughout his career and only served white patrons in his restaurant. Little did they know, he was hiding a dangerous secret in the basement.

Thomas Downing grew up on Virginia's Chincoteague Island, where his family made their living from the sea by fishing, clamming, and raking oysters. The skills Downing acquired during his childhood carried him to Philadelphia—he'd followed the troops north after the War of 1812—where he spent seven years running an oyster bar.

In the 1820s, most registered oystermen were African American, and opportunity in the industry was abundant, especially for people like Downing, who came from oyster-rich states along the Chesapeake Bay like Virginia. But the world's oyster capital was New York City, and Downing moved there, spending his days on a schooner harvesting oysters from the beds of the city's waters and selling them to restaurants or on the streets.

Joanne Hyppolite, culture curator at the National Museum of

African American History and Culture, first learned about Downing while researching the foodways section of the museum's Cultural Expressions exhibition. "He arrives in New York in 1819," she explains. "During that period, New York doesn't have an established fine dining industry or culture." But Downing had a vision that no one else shared, realizing he could make more money by elevating his space and offerings.

Top-dollar plates and fine dining usually come to mind when we think of oysters and the restaurants that serve them. But before New York loved hotdogs, oysters were the city's go-to street food for everyone regardless of race or class. Oystermen's stalls lined the streets of Manhattan, and for about six cents, you could get a dozen fried oysters. Then, there were the oyster refractories; rough-edged, cellar-like dives. Usually, a steep set of stairs led diners into a dimly lit space that wasn't well furnished and likely a bit crowded.

Dive bars and taverns were plentiful, but high-end restaurants like the oyster house didn't yet exist. NYC's beloved Italian steakhouse, Delmonico's, is often hailed as the first fine dining restaurant in the country, opening in 1827, or the United States Hotel in Philadelphia, which opened in 1826. Not only did Downing turn oysters into a delicacy, but he was also the first to dish out fine dining.

Thomas Downing's Oyster House opened in 1825 in the heart of the financial district. Downing's two adjoining properties sat on Broad Street, both roomy and beautifully dressed with interiors far more impressive than the usual cellars. Curtains graced the windows, crystal-crusted chandeliers hung above the dining area, and fine carpet covered the floors. The Oyster House oozed luxury and existed exclusively for the elite.

Before he opened his restaurant, Thomas Downing was well-known for being a canny curator of oysters. He would set out beneath crisp midnight air, following the glow of his lantern to the vessels of local oystermen, where he'd meticulously dig to the bottom of oyster piles to pick the best of the beds. Downing would always shell out top dollar to his comrades to ensure they continuously gave him the highest quality product.

Downing's rich taste didn't stop at the door. Everything was designed to delight and satisfy his clientele. "Ladies and gentlemen with towel in hand, and an English oyster knife made for the purpose, would open their own oysters, drop the burning hot concaved shell a lump of sweet butter and other seasonings, and partake of a treat," his son, George, wrote in an essay about his father in 1887.

Whether deliberate or not, the restaurant's premier location, next door to the Merchant's Exchange and the Customs House, was a wise choice and likely integral to Downing's place becoming the city's best-known oyster spot. His clientele was the upper crust: primarily white men with means. Some were bankers, others merchants, and many were dignitaries from all over the world visiting the US.

Before Downing entered the scene, women didn't dine in restaurants. It would have been considered uncouth. Downing changed that. His Oyster House was a respectable place where well-to-do husbands wanted to bring their families for dinner. The aristocrats and who's-who of New York wouldn't dare slurp oysters from anywhere else.

By the 1840s, business was booming, so much so that Downing began catering. He offered international mail-order shipping, sending raw, pickled, and fresh shells to Europe and fried oysters to the Caribbean. One of his most famous customers across the pond was Queen Victoria, who was a big fan of Downing's discerning taste. She loved his oysters so much that she sent him a gold chronometer watch as a thank you.

Downing was indeed becoming New York City's best. The city called on him to cater its legendary multimillion-dollar feast, the Boz Ball, held in 1842 to celebrate English writer Charles Dickens.

Perhaps the most delicious part of Thomas Downing's food story is the secret he hid beneath the feet of his elite clientele. Underneath the fancy floorboards of the Oyster House, Downing was not only storing shells and wine. Instead, he and young George also hid enslaved people fleeing the South to Canada, where they would be free.

Downing's place became one of the essential stops along the Underground Railroad, especially during a time when bounty hunters roamed New York's streets, seeking out those escaping from slavery in the South.

Despite his wealth, Downing himself experienced the indignity of white supremacy, culminating in an attack in 1838. "He was on several trolley cars that were segregated and refused to leave his seat, just like Rosa Parks," Hyppolite says. When Downing refused to move seats, others on the trolley ganged up to beat him. But unlike most Black people during the 1800s, he could afford to take his assailants to court.

Mourners poured in from the doors to the pulpit of St Philip's Episcopal Church when Thomas Downing, then well-known as the "oyster king of New York," died in 1866 at the age of 75. There was no doubt about what he meant to the city. Manhattan's top merchants loved Downing and wanted to attend his funeral, so in an unheard-of move, the New York Chamber of Commerce closed for the day. As the *New York Times* reported, on the day of Downing's wake, a "long line of carriages, well-filled with mourners" attended the ceremony, as well as multiple delegations of Freemasons "in full regalia."

On his father's death, George, a great activist and businessman himself, operated the New York oyster house until at least 1871. But Downing's own legacy as a restaurateur and an abolitionist resounds even today.

Soon, you'll even be able to try Downing-style oysters yourself. At the National Museum of African American History and Culture in Washington, D.C., Downing's story is displayed in the Cultural Expressions gallery and at the museum's Sweet Home Cafe.

In 2023, when the museum plans to once more offer a full menu at the cafe, Oyster Pan Roast will be there. This creamy bowl of oysters, blanketed by rich red butter sauce flavored with shallots, deglazed with white wine, and reduced with chili sauce and cream, is a delicious homage to Downing and his remarkable achievements.

CAROLINE HATCHETT

The Elusive Roots of Rosin Potatoes

FROM *Bitter Southerner*

DURING THE DECADES my hometown of Baxley, Georgia, hosted Tree Fest, men from Akzo Nobel, a chemical manufacturer with a local plant, would gather around a 6-foot-tall pot filled with 200 pounds of rosin. Led by Bo Herndon—a plant supervisor, former police chief, and father to my catechism classmate Heather—the team would bring the rosin to a vigorous simmer over a high-powered propane burner, and then drop in potatoes, 50 or so at a time. After 30 minutes, the potatoes would bob to the surface and Bo and Co. would pluck them out with tongs, wrap the potatoes— perilously sticky with molten rosin—in newspaper, and sell one of America's great culinary oddities for a buck or two.

I was oblivious to this culinary display. Tree Fest had other diversions: an early-morning fun run, funnel cake, vendors selling scented candles and Kiss My Grits T-shirts. My sister's Labrador, Dixie, won the pet costume contest three years in a row. I tapped with a troupe from the Gail Hursey School of Dance, and, one year, as a junior chamber of commerce volunteer, I roamed the fairgrounds dressed as Woody, the festival's pine tree mascot.

Pines meant something in Appling County. I grew up with slash pines towering over me and wheelbarrows' worth of pine cones in the yard. The trees would paint our driveway yellow with pollen in spring. Lightning would occasionally strike their crowns, and, with the immediate boom of thunder, every wall and window of our house would rattle.

My dad, Tom Hatchett, managed timberland for Union Camp and, later on, International Paper. My best friend Lindsay's dad worked at Rayonier, a plant just east of downtown with stacks of denuded pine trunks piled high in its yard. Pine trees brought our families to this part of rural south Georgia. And I couldn't wait to leave it.

Neither could Thurnell Alston, the protagonist in *Praying for Sheetrock*, Melissa Fay Greene's nonfiction account of McIntosh County's late-to-arrive Civil Rights Movement. Along with his father and a pickup truck full of men, Alston rode from the Georgia coast to inland piney woods to clear paths for other turpentine workers and deposit gum collected from the trees into barrels; they toiled from early morning until nightfall for monthlong stretches and slept in windowless shanties on the floor.

After six years of grueling, low-paid work, Alston literally walked off the job, trekking 60 miles on foot from Baxley to Brunswick. I read *Praying for Sheetrock* in late 2019 and mentioned Baxley's cameo to my dad. Sensing a rare connection in our work, he posed a question, some version of which I've since asked the living and the dead across 10 states and two countries: What do you know about rosin potatoes?

It's widely accepted that rosin potatoes hail from the South's turpentine camps, where workers chipped and slashed and scraped pine trees to collect oleoresin (aka resin or gum), the trees' natural defense mechanism. When a tree's bark is breached—by a beetle, fungus, or a woodsman's hack—it oozes gum, not sap, from the wound. When fossilized, oleoresin transforms into amber. When distilled, it yields turpentine and rosin, whose uses range from paint thinner and Vicks VapoRub to rubber cement and chewing gum, respectively.

The rosin potato origin story goes one of two ways. A hapless worker dropped a potato into hot rosin as it was coming off the still, and when the potato came to the surface, he pulled it out and found a perfectly cooked spud. Alternately, an industrious worker saw in molten rosin an efficient method for making a hot lunch.

Outside the context of the woods, cooking potatoes in rosin is a wholly impractical preparation.

Rosin is highly flammable, and its fumes are noxious. It requires a dedicated pot and tongs; there's no easy cleaning of hardened rosin. Oh—and you can't eat the potato's skin.

Despite those odds, the technique went mainstream in the 1950s and merited inclusion in James Beard's 1960 *Treasury of Outdoor Cooking* and in the 1975 edition of *The Joy of Cooking*. In 1976, rosin potatoes were on the table the night my parents got engaged at Art's Steakhouse in Gainesville, Florida, and Cracker Barrel served the potatoes from 1983 through 1991.

Rosin potato loyalists say the preparation yields a superior potato with a flaky texture. Just as oleoresin seals a tree's wounds, rosin traps a potato's flavor and aroma, according to chef Sean Brock, who included rosin potatoes on the debut menu at Audrey, his fine-dining restaurant in Nashville. "Because none of the potato's flavor or aroma compounds can escape, you get the most intense potato flavor you've ever experienced," Brock says. "And they're steaming in their own water, which is why you get a totally unique texture."

Outside of Audrey, you won't find rosin potatoes in many restaurants these days. Except in vintage cookbooks, Reddit forums, and a smattering of rural festivals, rosin potatoes all but disappeared from the American culinary canon.

In the summer of 2020, Dad drove to Patterson, Georgia, to pick up 25 pounds of rosin from Diamond G Forest Products, a boutique producer of gum rosin and turpentine. I drove from New York to Baxley. In his garage, with the door rolled open, we fired up a propane cooker, melted rosin, and dropped in potatoes. The fumes coming off the pot were piney and potent, enough to make you dizzy in the heat, so I stood back, bare feet on smooth concrete, watching as a fury of bubbles rose from the swampy liquid. A half-hour into the boil, the potatoes began to emerge one by one.

But it would take another year for their origins to surface. Turpentiners did not record the grand discovery that is rosin potatoes, or from where, exactly, they hail.

They left that up to me.

A Modern Product from an Age-Old Tree

In the history of humanity, rosin is a relatively modern product. Before it came tar and pitch, derived from European birch and pine at least 10,000 years ago. Ancient Greeks and Vikings used pine tar to waterproof their ships. In Genesis, God tells Noah,

"Make yourself an ark out of resinous wood. Make it of reeds, and caulk it with pitch inside and out."

By the 17th century, England needed a new source of tar, pitch, and turpentine—a trinity of supplies known as naval stores that would coat, seal, and preserve the Royal Navy's ropes and ships. The world superpower had produced the stuff on an industrial scale since at least the Middle Ages, but as its forest resources thinned, England turned to Prussia and Sweden, and eventually to the American Colonies, for its naval stores.

The Carolinas had seemingly endless stretches of longleaf pine and soil ill-suited for cash crops and by 1725 produced a net surplus of tar, pitch, and turpentine. By the mid-19th century, North Carolina's naval stores industry was booming, with the state boasting nearly 800 stills and operators producing more than $5 million ($185 million today) of gum and turpentine. That wealth and labor, of course, was derived at the expense of enslaved workers, of whom we know little aside from their impact on plantation balance sheets.

Plantations hired out enslaved people to turpentine operations for up to $250 a year at the industry's height. Swinging giant axes, these men would box 75 to 100 trees a day, or around 10,000 trees each winter, and chip 1,000–2,000 faces a day. (Faces, or catfaces, are the areas from which bark has been hacked off and rosin flows.) They were housed in dirt-floor lean-tos and issued daily rations of salt pork, cornmeal, and, yes, potatoes. One of the few advantages these men had over enslaved plantation farm workers was their ability to supplement their diets with wild foods like fish, turtle, raccoon, and possum.

If these workers ate rosin potatoes, we do not know it. Rosin, at this point, had little commercial value. Rather than paying to ship it, producers let it run off the still onto the land and into waterways. When Frederick Law Olmsted toured North Carolina turpentine operations in the early 1850s, he observed "a congealed pool of rosin, estimated to contain over three thousand barrels," according to his *A Journey in the Seaboard Slave States*.

I looked to historical accounts like Olmsted's and expected, at any moment, for rosin potatoes to leap off the pages.

In the seminal *Tapping the Pines*, Robert Outland introduces Sarah Hicks Williams, the wife of a North Carolina turpentiner, whose letters detail meals of cornbread, biscuits, sweet potatoes, peaches, apples, and vinegar-dressed pork barbecue—but no rosin potatoes.

I hoped to find them on plantation menus and checked with folks at the Bellamy Mansion in Wilmington, North Carolina. The 10,000-square-foot home was built by John D. Bellamy, a merchant, farmer, and turpentine operator, who owned 115 enslaved workers, 24 of whom labored at his turpentine camp in Columbus County. The family's elaborate Christmas menus included duck, roast pig, rutabagas hashed with Irish potatoes, brandy peaches, coconut pie, and syllabub (sweetened curdled milk), but there's no rosin on the menu, nor records of what Bellamy's enslaved workers ate at camp.

"No one was keeping good records," Outland told me. "It's hard to write about a life when they were considered unimportant people."

Outland, who lives in North Carolina, spent the summer of 1996 driving across the southeastern United States, researching the dissertation that would become *Tapping the Pines*. He combed archives, knocked on doors, and held rosin in his hands for the first time. Nowhere in his fieldwork did he encounter rosin potatoes.

"There was fire everywhere around backwoods processing facilities. Why not roast potatoes? People really were struggling out there in the woods," Outland says. "I don't know who got it in their head, but it seems to be human nature, looking back with rosy glasses at the past. They imagined an old-time turpentine lifestyle and invented a way to celebrate it."

After its mid-19th-century boom, the Tar Heel State (named after a slur associated with turpentine workers) saw its naval stores industry decline rapidly. Between 1840 and 1893, more than 90% of North Carolina's longleaf pine forest had been boxed, destroyed, and abandoned. In turn, operators moved to the virgin forests of South Carolina, Alabama, Mississippi, Georgia, and Florida.

But it was south Georgia—in particular, on land between the Savannah and Chattahoochee rivers—that would supplant North Carolina as the nation's naval stores capital.

In the decades leading up to the Civil War, turpentiners transplanted entire plantation populations to Georgia's piney woods, and migration continued at an even more rapid pace after the war. Newly emancipated Black workers followed the industry, having few other choices, and by the late 19th century the average Georgia turpentine worker was a "young, single, illiterate, Black man from North Carolina," Outland wrote in *Tapping the Pines.*

Baxley was transformed by turpentine into a rural engine of the South's economy, and in ways I could not comprehend, turpentine wealth, power, and culture steeped themselves into my upbringing.

Abandoned turpentine shacks, unpainted and with tin roofs and front porches caving in, dotted county roads. In downtown Baxley, there's a four-columned white mansion off U.S. 1 with a tennis court in the backyard; it always looked too fancy for the town and was owned by Edgar Dyal, a turpentine magnate. The tracks that slice Baxley in two were part of the Macon and Brunswick Railroad, built to haul naval stores and lumber to the coast. Lewis Parker, Appling County's sheriff for 20 years, hailed from the Veal family, one of the county's biggest naval stores producers. And when the last bucket of American pine gum was dipped for commercial use by Major Phillips, he delivered it from Soperton, Georgia, to Baxley for distillation at Akzo Nobel, the last U.S. processor of gum rosin.

Early in my potato hunt, my dad introduced me to Bill Baker, a retired Akzo Nobel engineer and plant manager. Baker's granddaddy had timber stands and a fire still out near the Veals', and though he expected to leave town for good, rosin cemented Baker in place. He started working at Filtered Rosin Products in the mid-'60s and stuck around as the plant was sold to Akzo Nobel in the '80s and, eventually, to two investment groups.

"We made products from rosin from living pine trees. There are other rosins made from paper mills, where they grind pulp and extract it with sulphuric acid. That rosin, you don't want to use for potatoes," explains Baker, who over the years entertained visiting businesspeople with steak and rosin potato dinners.

He doesn't remember where he first learned about the dish, but the story Baker has heard and told for decades rings true: "Turpentine workers would be collecting rosin from the fire still. They'd have hot rosin in barrels, and around noon, they'd throw potatoes in the barrel and let them cook."

In 1981, the Georgia Museum of Agriculture built a turpentine still complete with an antique copper kettle, and every April, David King, the museum's superintendent of restoration and maintenance, fires the still. Just off 1–75 in Tifton, the living history museum is one of the few places in the country where you can see pine gum transformed into turpentine and rosin and eat potatoes cooked in hot-off-the-still rosin.

My dad and I met King, a little sunburned and with graying hair tucked under a camouflage cap, in a giant, shadeless parking lot, and he led us back to the nine-barrel still, encased in red brick and sheltered under a rustic two-story wooden structure. Workers would roll barrels of gum to the top and tip the contents into the still. The steam, containing water and spirits of turpentine, would rise through a pipe and then wind through copper tubing set inside a cypress water tank. Once condensed, the solution would flow into a barrel and turpentine would rise to the top. At the end of distillation, workers opened a chute at the bottom of the still and rosin gushed out through screens and cotton batting and into a trough. Men with long-handled dippers would then transfer the filtered rosin into barrels.

Standing next to the still—the ground in front of it puddled with semi-firm rosin—was like going to church. It made me want to believe. Just as Baker knows the rosin business, King has mastered the mechanics of 19th-century production, working with old-timers and historians and firing stills five or so times a year. He sent me home with hunks of rosin, new leads to call, and a glimmer of hope that I'd find the potatoes in south Georgia.

From Turpentine Camps to Industry Parties
At the end of "A Longleaf Legacy," a 2018 documentary about the industry, Buster Cole, a still worker and interpreter for the Georgia Museum of Agriculture, extemporaneously calls out varied rosin uses: "gunpowder, glass, fiberglass, acrylics, polyester, chewing gum, costume jewelry, tile, carpet, Elmer's glue, shellac, shoe polish, soap, sprinkle it on your dance floor to make it slick, they make nine cosmetics out of it and three perfumes out of it. Gymnastics you got a rosin bag, bowling you got a rosin bag, tennis you got a rosin bag. Baseball pitcher, he use a rosin bag, fiddler put rosin on his bow, ballet dancer put it on their shoes. . . ."

Having visited the still and watching the video, I hoped Cole would blurt out, "And you can even cook a potato in it." But he didn't.

Folklorist Laurie Sommers founded the South Georgia Folklife Project at Valdosta State University and, with Tim Prizer, interviewed dozens of turpentine workers with multigenerational ties to the industry, such as George "G.W." Harrington, a man born into the business. Harrington's father managed 16,000 acres of forest, and his mother helped run the camp commissary. "Mama believed in a hot meal," he told Sommers in 2004, recalling Friday-night fish fries and the scent of greens, sweet potatoes, and homemade biscuits wafting through the camp.

According to Harrington, a typical day's menu in the 1940s and '50s consisted of grits, fried eggs, bacon, and oatmeal for breakfast; dinner (aka lunch) meant "something that would stick with you" like fried chicken, rice, speckled butter beans, cornbread, corn, okra, new potatoes, sliced tomatoes, biscuits, and some kind of dessert; for supper, the family ate leftovers or country sausage.

Most workers' lunches were more humble affairs, according to Sommers, like cornbread or canned salmon with rice and beans, carried in cane syrup cans and hung from trees.

"There is no way something as unusual and fascinating as rosin potato would be something that flew under the radar and was forgotten," says Prizer, who went on to write his master's thesis on nostalgia and memory in the waning days of the industry.

But none of Sommers' or Prizer's subjects mentioned the potatoes. They're similarly omitted from Carroll Butler's *Treasures of the Longleaf Pines*, notable for being the only scholarly book on the industry produced by a former turpentiner, and Pete Gerrell's *The Illustrated History of the Naval Stores (Turpentine) Industry*.

Both works are a feast of food details. Butler describes lunches of hoe cakes and doobie (a savory cobbler relative), as well as workers hunting for rabbit, squirrel, raccoon, and gopher tortoise. He also describes backwoods booze, including "alcohol strained from Sterno and then mixed with sugar water and spirits of niter [ethyl nitrite]." Gerrell shares recipes for cottage beer, pigs feet, and Spanish moss jelly. "You know that times are bad when there is nothing left to eat but Spanish moss seasoned with fish bladder," he wrote.

Gerrell and Butler are both deceased, as are all but one or two of the folks interviewed by Sommers and Prizer. But as a daughter of one of the last important turpentine cities, I hoped I might find living workers—and rosin potato camp stories—in Baxley.

James Copeland tapped trees in Appling County until 1960, and his family line extends back to North Carolina. His father farmed tobacco and cotton and collected gum on his own land, in addition to working faces for another operator. "There was a man he worked for, probably 25 or 35 years. My grandfather worked for that man's daddy doing turpentine. The first work I did, as far back as I can remember, was farm work and turpentine," Copeland says.

Copeland is married to Pearl Copeland, who was raised on the Veals' turpentine farm and whose brother and father worked in the business. Pearl is an accomplished country cook. She was making a jelly cake the last time we spoke and promised a feast of fried chicken, lima beans, cornbread, blackberry pie, peach pie, and pear pie the next time I come home.

The Copelands had never heard of rosin potatoes.

Pearl recalls folks cooking sweet potatoes under a pile of sand with a fire built on top. James took cold potatoes into the forest and field, but more often lunch was a biscuit sandwich with bacon, peanut butter and homemade jelly, or a smear of preserved pear, packed in a syrup can.

"You didn't heat no food up. Whatever you left home with, by the time you eat it, it's cold," he says. "When you ate, there wasn't nothing like . . . take an hour for lunch."

They were incredulous that the technique would even work. "I don't know nobody in Appling County who could tell you about that," Pearl told me. "That somebody who was telling you the way they did it, they were saying something that was untrue."

The Copelands' experience working family land and trees represents the zenith of the industry for Black workers, who sold gum to central distilleries as supplemental income. But before Civil Rights legislation passed in the 1960s, the Jim Crow South held a significant number of Black turpentine workers in bondage through debt peonage, most often by forcing them to buy marked-up goods at camp commissaries. Though the practice was illegal at the federal level, Southern states enacted laws that forbade workers from leaving jobs while indebted to their bosses.

The industry also leased convicts—a majority being Black men—from the state. Though it had been outlawed elsewhere, Georgia and Florida practiced convict leasing until 1908 and 1923, respectively.

Though Prizer found relationships between some owners and Black workers were warm, respectful, and often nuanced, anyone poking through turpentine's past will find, in abundance, brutality, kidnapping, coercion, paternalism, and searing racism.

The more I poked and dug and read, I could not understand why a Black worker in the Jim Crow South would cook his lunch in rosin, a commodity product whose value was determined by its clarity. Were workers really dropping dirty potatoes into rosin that had been distilled and filtered through cotton batting and screens? It sounded like a punishable offense.

By this point, I had grown mighty suspicious—like, rosin-potatogate conspiracy theory suspicious. With no collective memory—written, recorded, or alive—of rosin potatoes in turpentine camps, I turned my attention away from workers and toward the industry, the big-wigs, moneymakers, and political influencers who might have something to gain from rosin potatoes.

At the University of Florida's Smathers Libraries, I hunched over volumes of *Naval Stores Review*, following two-plus decades of industry exploits. Published weekly from 1890 to 1953 (and later monthly and bimonthly), the *Review* provides a play-by-play of the industry's swings, technological advances, best practices, politics, labor woes, and evolving culture. Its pages instructed producers how to convert from harmful box cutting to installing metal gutters and ceramic Herty cups, a method that prolonged trees' viability and allowed the once mobile industry to put down roots. It doc-umented the move from backwoods distilling to central stills in towns like Baxley, the rise of acid sprays to increase gum produc-tion, and every possible use for turpentine and rosin—from soap production in Peru to home insulation, cough syrup, and a depila-tory for pigs.

The *Naval Stores Review* also chronicled the American Turpen-tine Farmers Association, or AT-FA, formed in 1936 and led by Judge Harley Langdale, a powerful naval stores producer and politician from Valdosta, Georgia.

AT-FA loomed large over the industry's fading years. Members funded successful national ad campaigns and an effort to get gum turpentine onto retail shelves. The organization supported research and lobbied to classify turpentiners as agricultural workers, ex-empting producers from minimum wage laws and Social Security taxes. AT-FA administered a federal loan program that sought to limit naval stores production and stabilize market prices. They also threw one helluva party.

Each April, more than a thousand producers and their families would gather in Valdosta for the annual AT-FA Convention. Langdale would rally turpentiners behind the cause of the moment and conjure the industry's demise if action was not taken, and then get voted in as president for another term.

"The gum industry faces able, aggressive, and intelligent competition from many new spirits companies. This competition must be met by the gum industry or the industry will be swallowed up by it," he told attendees in 1947.

They'd host a stag-night fish fry for the men, along with a beauty contest in which women dressed in longleaf pine needle bikinis. The weekend would conclude with a picnic featuring 700 barbecued chickens (and ham in later years), peas, grits, potato salad, beer, and Coca-Cola. In 1949, they switched up the menu and harvested Florida sabal palms to make swamp cabbage.

Had the rosin potato existed in naval stores culture, it should've been at that barbecue. Just as Langdale wrapped his arm around each Miss Spirits of Turpentine, he would have been pulling a potato out of the rosin pot for a photo op. Rosin potatoes were also absent from Swainsboro's Pine Tree Festival, from industry conferences, and from field trips to the Naval Stores Research Station in Olustee, Florida, a hub of scientific advancement for the industry. Starting with the year 1933, I flipped page by page, year by year, through the *Naval Stores Review*, expecting to meet the potato at any moment. And there was nothing—until June 1956.

The year before, N.J. "Jack" Stallworth, whose brother was an AT-FA director, had demonstrated rosin baked potatoes at the Alabama State Fair. Stallworth served the potatoes in his Mobile, Alabama, restaurant, Stafills, and advertised direct-to-consumer rosin in pamphlets, as well as in *Gourmet, Living,* and *House Beautiful. Naval Stores Review* did not credit Stallworth or anyone in particular with the invention, but noted, "Rosin baked potatoes is not an entirely new idea, having been initiated some two years ago."

In other words, folks in the industry had not eaten rosin potatoes, a "Southern delicacy" as they called them, until 1954. They didn't associate the newfangled technique with turpentine camp culture, nor did they know when or where the potatoes had been invented.

Making Headlines

Rosin potatoes first appeared in print in April 1939 in a syndicated dispatch from Damon Runyon, a journalist best known for writing *Guys and Dolls.* "We recently came across a brand new way of cooking white potatoes. You boil them in resin—the same kind of resin that violinists rub on their bowstrings and also the very same kind of resin prizefighters shuffle the soles of their shoes in," wrote Runyon, attributing the dish to Black Caesar's Forge, a restaurant in Miami. "The Dade County folks love to introduce their Yankee friends to the ceremony."

Later that year, Charles H. Baker, a Florida-born bon vivant and writer, published *The Gentleman's Companion: Exotic Cookery Book,* a collection of recipes of "manly dishes for men" according to the *Miami Herald.* In it, he shared a recipe for "Rosin Potatoes in the Manner of J. Marquette Phillips as Done at Black Caesar's Forge for Various Friends & Guests, at Various Times." Those guests, according to Baker, included senators, poet Robert Frost, and actor Errol Flynn.

Black Caesar's Forge opened in 1938, 15 miles south of downtown Miami in Palmetto Bay. Named for a legendary pirate rumored to have buried treasure on the Miami coast, the restaurant's sunken dining room was carved into coral rock and lined with wine bins. In the early years, guests brought their own steaks, salad fixings, and potatoes, which Phillips charged a fee to grill, toss with a house vinaigrette, and drop in a rosin pot, respectively. "The problem in World War II was you couldn't get steak," says David Phillips, J. Marquette's grandson. "These were people with connections."

Phillips had moved from Detroit to Miami in 1925 at the height of a south Florida real estate boom. The place was warm, notoriously wet despite Prohibition, and accessible by rail line, and wealthy snowbirds built mansions and flocked to newly minted hotels on South Beach. Phillips established himself as a furniture importer and decorative iron worker, and you can still see his handiwork at mansions built by Harvey S. Firestone and William K. Vanderbilt II.

Phillips' business survived a series of devastating hurricanes and the 1929 stock market crash, and he built a South Beach home with a storefront and studio—and likely a speakeasy. After Prohibition's repeal, and with the support of wealthy patrons, Phillips transformed the space into The Forge Club, a nightclub, casino, and steakhouse decorated with intricate iron grilles and palm trees. He sold the club in 1942, and it operated as The Forge, an iconic Miami steakhouse, until closing in 2019.

By the time Black Caesar's Forge came around, Phillips had considerable social capital, and his potatoes were a local hit. Miamians added rosin potato hearths to their outdoor terraces. Snowbirds transported the potatoes back to their home states. Francis Kinney and Alberta Paskvan both served as World War II pilots, and, in the years after the war, met and married in Miami, where they frequented Black Caesar's Forge. After moving to Michigan and, later, Montana, they continued to cook rosin potatoes over a wood fire in the backyard, and often for a crowd of bewildered neighbors. "For my whole life, they were part of our family's cuisine," says their son Will Kinney, a theoretical cosmologist at the University of Buffalo and avid rosin potato maker. (Kinney cooks his potatoes for 20 additional minutes after they rise to the surface of the pot, for optimal texture.)

Rosin potatoes' popularity surged as families like the Kinneys moved to the suburbs and America's backyard barbecue culture took root. Hamilton and Abercrombie & Fitch, among other manufacturers, started selling rosin potato kits complete with a pot, an aluminum stand, and rosin.

With wartime rations lifted and celebrations in order, steakhouses flourished, and plenty of them added rosin potatoes to their menus. My grandparents ate them in Palm Beach in the '50s, when rosin potatoes had gourmet connotations. At a 1953 gathering of Les Amis d'Escoffier, "a band of real gourmets" ate rosin potatoes alongside bouillon, clams casino, oysters Rockefeller, caviar, crawfish quenelles, wild mallard, and Champagne.

There was no turpentine camp narrative at this point. Just as AT-FA promoted the newness and novelty of the preparation, so did the national press. But that started to change as rosin potatoes established themselves in the South and in turpentine strongholds. Soon they were on menus at the Mayflower Hotel in Jacksonville; Heritage Inn in Columbia, South Carolina; the Pirates' House in Savannah; and Coyner's in Macon, Georgia. Rosin potatoes were also a specialty of notoriously racist Aunt Fanny's Cabin in Smyrna, Georgia. By the '70s, the rosin potato myth had cemented and Planters Back Porch Seafood Restaurant in Myrtle Beach, South Carolina, told the tall tale on its menu:

"Many years ago a worker in a turpentine plant dropped a raw potato into an iron vat of bubbling hot rosin. The potato sank out of sight . . . but some 20 minutes later suddenly reappeared floating on the surface of the heavy rosin. The worker took a large ladle and scooped the potato out of the rosin and after curiosity got the better of him, he cut the potato open and proceeded to enjoy the most delicious potato ever before baked. Word of this culinary find circulated throughout the pine belt of the South and soon practically every plantation in the land had its own rosin pot out back for cooking the famous 'rosin-taters.'"

The rosin potato had outgrown Black Caesar's Forge and taken on a whole new identity, but Phillips had already moved on. He sold the restaurant in 1946 and settled in Cuba, where he ran a 35,000-acre fruit, mining, and timber plantation. Fidel Castro's government seized the land in 1960, and Phillips died six years later.

Phillips never claimed to have invented the potato. He told friends and reporters he had seen it elsewhere but never revealed his source. There's a chance he witnessed the potato cookery in central or northern Florida, where his wife Edna Valentine Paul's family operated a lumber business. But there's not a lick of proof rosin potatoes existed in the deep woods, and if they did, I can't believe J. Marquette Phillips was the sole person to have brought them to the public's attention.

On the contrary, I think he was concealing the potato's backstory.

Steak and (Rosin) Potatoes

Outside the industry, resin and pitch—the latter made by cooking down oleoresin until thick and sticky—often are used interchangeably. At a certain point last summer, and on a desperate whim, I typed "pitch potatoes" into a newspaper archive. The first dozen or so hits were commodity lists; pitch and potatoes follow each other alphabetically. But then I found exactly what I was looking for: rosin potatoes' predecessor boiling in the pots of Cincinnati's pre-Prohibition German-American breweries.

By the mid-19th century, Cincinnati was home to a thriving beer industry whose German brewers were no strangers to pitch. In his 1829 *The Art of Brewing*, writer David Booth details the distinctly German practice of lining barrels with pitch to prevent contamination, leakage, and the transference of wood's flavor and color into beer.

The 1850s and '60s also coincided with the rise of pale lagers, a style of beer invented just a few years earlier at Pilsner Urquell in the Czech Republic. Lager means "storeroom" in German, and requires brewing and conditioning at cold temperatures. Modern light lagers are brewed year-round and age in refrigerated storage tanks, typically for 10 days to a month, but before commercial refrigeration, Cincinnati breweries made lager in the winter months, placed the barrels in deep cellars, dropped in ice harvested from frozen lakes and rivers, added straw or sawdust for insulation, and sealed it all with pitch. That way, crisp, fresh lagers flowed all summer long.

"Breweries were going through radical changes in the lager era," says Mike Morgan, a Cincinnati beer historian and author of *Over-the-Rhine: When Beer Was King*. "You have to have these big lagering cellars. So brewing goes from something you can start on a small scale to digging a four-story hole and building over the top of it this brewery that would cost tens of millions of dollars today. Capital gets shifted, the spaces are a lot larger, and brewers are more concerned with politics."

It's in this environment that pitch potatoes, cooked in the same manner as rosin potatoes, have their moment in Cincinnati. The oldest reference I've found to pitch potatoes is from 1892 at a lunch hosted at a social club associated with the Christian Moerlein Brewing Co. According to a note in the *Cincinnati Enquirer*, "John Moerlein gave a 'pitch' potato lunch at the Elm Street Club rooms yesterday afternoon to a party of friends. It was quite a novel affair, and was heartily enjoyed."

The *Enquirer*'s casual mention of the dish, with no elaboration on the cooking method, suggests readers were already familiar with the potatoes, and Morgan believes they could date back as far as the 1870s. But it was at late-19th-century beefsteak dinners—a raucous style of dining and political campaigning that originated in New York City—that pitch potatoes flourished. To court votes and favors, raise campaign funds, and reward political donors, boosters and clubs would throw hours-long, all-you-can-eat steak dinners. In Cincinnati, breweries often played host, hanging chandeliers, setting up white-linened tables, and letting amber fluid flow freely, according to Morgan.

While bread was the carbohydrate of choice in New York, Cincinnati embraced the pitch potato. In addition to the John Kauffman Brewing Company, where "steaks were broiled over the coke fires in the malt dryers, and were served with 'pitch' potatoes and other vegetables," the potatoes were a fixture at the Bellevue, Mohawk, Windisch-Muhlhauser, Lackman, Buckeye, Jackson, Wiedmann's, and Bruckmann breweries.

Beefsteak dinners didn't have an exclusive hold on pitch potatoes. They were served in the city's beer gardens. In its 1904/1905 *Sigma Chi Quarterly*, frat boys visiting Chester Park, an amusement complex, recorded "an open-air dinner, spread upon the longest tables I have ever seen—one hundred yards if an inch: a dinner consisting of potatoes cooked in tar and served in round balls of paper, and many other strange and awful edibles and things."

Turn-of-the-century Cincinnati was also a major hub for conferences and conventions, of which pitch potatoes were a feature. At the 1898 gathering of the Master Horseshoers' National Protective Association, 350 members, representing 130 cities, ate a pitch potato supper. The Iron and Steel Workers' Convention of 1906 featured a beefsteak and pitch potato dinner, as did a 1909 gathering of 2,000 Knights of Pythias, a post–Civil War fraternal organization. In 1913, the National Association of Trunk Manufacturers ate pitch potatoes at Wiedmann's. In 1910, the Cincinnati Elks chapter threw a "beefsteak and pitch potato feast" for Elks en route to a convention in Detroit.

The preparation also emerged in cities like Buffalo and Pittsburgh. But almost as suddenly as pitch potatoes rose from the newspaper archives, they vanished again.

When World War I broke out in 1914, so did anti-German hysteria. Ohio, once a bilingual state, declared English its official language and banned German language classes in schools before eighth grade. German street names changed. The press renamed sauerkraut "liberty cabbage" and hamburger "liberty steak." The Espionage Act of 1917 explicitly outlawed interfering with military operations and recruitment and essentially outlawed anything un-American, aka German.

"That was the death blow," Morgan says. Cincinnati's German clubs, almost infinite in number, disbanded. Prohibition finished the job. Shifting to near-beer production, Bruckmann Brewery was the only Cincinnati brewery that operated from 1920 to 1933, and only six breweries reopened after states repealed the 18th Amendment. Pitch potatoes did not survive the upheaval.

By the time rosin potatoes made a national splash in the 1950s, most—but not all—Cincinnatians had forgotten pitch potatoes. I found one article, from 1955, in which a Cincinnati journalist connects zeitgeist-y rosin potatoes with "brewery days when kegs were lined with rosin," and at least one enterprising Cincinnati family continued to make the potatoes at home.

David Hackman, whose father, Arnold, was head brewer at Hudepohl Brewing Company, remembers eating the potatoes, along with steak and corn on the cob, as far back as 1947. He and his father built a brick structure in the backyard so they could melt pitch in a kettle over wood. Hackman eventually upgraded to propane, which provided a heat so intense it scarred a nearby magnolia tree. Still, something got lost in translation. Hackman cooks his potatoes in petroleum-based pitch, a substance that scares away skeptical friends and children. "This is my tar thing," says Hackman, insisting, "the worst thing to happen is you get black shit between your teeth."

Hackman, who's now 84, can claim something that no one else his age in the turpentine belt can: he grew up with pitch potatoes and can trace the dish's provenance. At least up to a point.

Pitch potatoes were bobbing around so many Cincinnati breweries, it's not clear where they originated. There's a single blog post on the internet linking the potatoes back to Germany, but it's a fuzzy connection at best.

I sent queries to a German-American beer scholar, a German food historian, and the Berlin-based Society for the History of Brewing, a collective of more than 300 members who research and publish German beer histories and maintain an archive and library. None had ever come across pitch potatoes in their research, nor had a beer museum in Thuringia, a region once known for producing exceptional brewers pitch.

There's perhaps one clue in a 1912 article in *Tägliches Cincinnatier Volksblatt*. Though the article is written in Old German, the words "pitch potatoes" appear in English, as if there's no direct translation. The piece concerns the visit of Gustav Stresemann from Dresden to Cincinnati. Stresemann would go on to serve as Germany's chancellor and win the Nobel Peace Prize, but at the time he served as executive director of Germany's Federation of Industrialists. The son of a beer distributor, Stresemann, who wrote his Ph.D. on beer bottling, wanted to visit a brewery while he was in town, and Windisch-Muhlhauser extended an invitation.

"Yet this was on such short notice that they could not offer pitch potatoes and steak but only bread, sausage, and ham, along with beer. They thought pitch potatoes were a delicious thing they should serve this grand dignitary," explained Jana Weiss, a beer historian at the University of Münster, who translated the article for me. "They would almost surely have used a German term if there was one."

I doubt I'll ever know for sure, but I believe pitch potatoes originated in Cincinnati breweries, where pitch was abundant and brewers found creative ways to cook with what they had on-site. At some point, J. Marquette Phillips came in contact with the dish, perhaps while traveling through Cincinnati or Pittsburgh, serving with Cincinnati men during World War I, or hobnobbing with Cincinnati snowbirds in Miami. But because his rosin potatoes debuted during World War II, Phillips chose not to disclose their German origins.

There's the possibility of parallel development, sure—the idea that the potato could have arisen independently in Cincinnati and the South. But I don't buy it. We know what turpentiners ate. It was recorded and passed down over centuries, and their foodways are alive today in homes like the Copelands'. What's quite clear is that while the early naval stores industry greedily consumed longleaf pines, German-American breweries were buying Southern-made pitch, feasting on potatoes cooked in it, and sharing it broadly with the public.

The rosin potato is weird. It's wild. It's captivating. It's also a pain in the ass. At both points in history when the rosin (née pitch) potato emerges, it hitches onto bigger cultural phenomena and explodes in popularity, only to recede into obscurity.

German-Americans had more potent traditions and symbols. They gave us Budweiser! Phillips thought of himself on a grand scale; after he was ejected from Cuba, he sent a letter to President Kennedy asking to be installed as an ambassador to a small Central or South American nation. Rosin potatoes were a mere side note in a colorful life.

Rosin potatoes never merited serious thought in the South precisely because they did not matter in the culture. They had little commercial value to the AT-FA crowd. Akzo Nobel sold 20,000 pounds of rosin a month to Cracker Barrel, according to Baker, but shipped out millions of pounds more of its rosin-based products to other buyers. Only when the naval stores industry cratered and its real traditions—the songs, camps, catfaces, and stills of the piney woods—started to disappear did folks latch on to rosin potatoes.

What Food Can Become

In May, I flew to Nashville to eat Sean Brock's pine rosin potato at Audrey. As part of the snack course on a tasting menu that was upwards of a C-note, servers presented (for visual devouring only) gorgeous, lacquered Appalachian Gold potatoes that had been boiled in rosin and set in a ceramic bowl atop pine needles. After those were whisked away, diners got a tiny bowl filled with rosin-cooked potato flesh mixed with local Cruze Farm buttermilk and topped with fresh trout roe and freeze-dried buttermilk.

Brock told me rosin, and its pine aroma, reminds him of growing up in Appalachia, and on Instagram he had called the potatoes an "old mountain tradition." That night at dinner, I told him I would be setting the record straight. These potatoes don't hail from Appalachia; they're not even from the South.

But in a bite, with pure potato flavor lit through with buttermilk tang, I recognized an unmistakable Southern accent.

Rosin potatoes may not hail from the South, but potatoes, when boiled in Southern-made rosin, are a portal that can both flatten and complicate the history of the naval stores industry—an industry that transformed whole regions, extracted wealth at the expense of Black workers, replaced longleaf ecosystems with slash pine farms, and, especially in later years, put groceries on the table and gave men purposeful work.

The faith folks have in rosin potatoes isn't just an act of blind, unquestioning nostalgia. In Tim Prizer's work with turpentiners, he writes, "It is clear that nostalgia is often productive, insightful, critical—even progressive. . . . From turpentine's material remains, former workers are able to extract profound experiential meaning, evaluate the current state of their communities, and determine which aspects of the past are worth transmitting into the future, which virtues of history should be upheld for posterity."

The rosin potato myth, as rosy as it is, imagines a world in which there was greater parity between white and Black turpentiners, that men working at the stills would break to share a hot lunch, a potato cooked in the literal fruits of their labor. And this potato would have been so exceptional that it would be replicated in restaurants and backyards across the country.

"The rosin potato fortifies [turpentiners'] own history," Prizer tells me, confessing that he, too, hadn't thought twice about the turpentine-camp origin story. "It makes their own past and the region's past more interesting, more alive, through this unusual food tradition, a food made from this thing that was their livelihood."

The first time I spoke with Bill Baker, he told me he felt proud every time he drove by Akzo Nobel. In it, he saw a lifetime of honest work with the living pine. Likewise, what the rest of the world sees as a truly strange potato preparation, turpentiners recognize and taste as the work of their hands.

What is Southern cuisine, Brock asked me at dinner, if not a combination of cultural influences, geography, and ingredients? "I'm mostly interested in what Southern food can become," he says. "Because it's about discovery. And what if everything hasn't been discovered?"

In 1991, the year Cracker Barrel discontinued the rosin potato, the restaurant chain offered a free dinner to anyone with "written proof of the use of recipes for rosin-baked potatoes before 1958." They didn't include a deadline for submissions, and I expect to collect on my comped plate of chicken and dumplings soon. In the same spirit, I'd love to buy a beer or dinner at Audrey for the first person with written proof of rosin, or pitch, potatoes before 1892.

Detroit's Chinatown and Gayborhood Felt Like Two Separate Worlds. Then They Collided

FROM *Bon Appétit*

DETROIT'S CHINATOWN WAS filled with old single men.

Most of them worked in food service as waiters and cooks—grueling jobs but the best they could get with their limited English skills. After long days they would arrive at my family's restaurant, Chung's Cantonese Cuisine, and practically sprint down a rickety back flight of stairs to the gambling den below. From the top of the landing, I could hear them swearing in Cantonese while casting their well-worn dominoes and chipped mah-jongg tiles. Occasionally, the gamblers would come up for a pair of our made-from-scratch cabbage egg rolls. If they were winning big, they'd splurge on a jumbo shrimp cocktail.

The disproportionately large number of men seemed odd to me until my parents explained how America's immigration policies had long prevented Chinese women from entering the country. Why? Presumably out of the unfounded fear that their America would be replaced by hordes of yellow people. Though the U.S. tried to correct this imbalance starting in the 1940s, the gender disparity persisted in cities like Detroit well into the '80s. Seeking kinship, these dozens of men from southern China formed their own chosen family, a bachelor society centered on the tong, an organization that oversaw the safety and welfare of the local Chinese community—but was sometimes associated with organized crime. Despite the negative stereotypes, these guys seemed more like harmless, cranky uncles to me.

Meanwhile, surrounding Chinatown was Detroit's gay community, filled with young single white men.

These men weren't facing any laws preventing them from being with women. They just preferred the company of other men, ones with nicely trimmed haircuts, six-pack abs, and Burt Reynolds mustaches. Plus, they ran businesses I'd never seen in Chinatown, like a pet store, a dog-grooming service, and an antique shop stacked with *Life* magazines. They even had a bar with a sign touting their entertainment of "female impersonators"—I had no idea what that was, but it sounded really intriguing to me.

As a curious 12-year-old, I often snuck off to Birdtown, the colorful pet store. Through rows of blue-tinted lights illuminating 10-gallon tanks filled with black-and-white angelfish and orange swordtails, I'd eavesdrop on the pet shop boys as they chatted around the register, flipping through their Hollywood gossip magazines.

At that age I had already recognized that a part of me belonged to each group of men. But I also knew I had to keep these worlds separate. It's not that either disparaged the other—no one in Chinatown said anything homophobic and no one in the gayborhood said anything anti-Asian. But growing up in our segregated city, bathing in pervasive, casual bigotry on my school playground, I didn't want to create any unnecessary drama in either community. I felt at home in both worlds but was scared of what might happen if they collided.

It was the end of the night and Chung's had welcomed a big table of visiting VIPs, elderly men in ill-fitting suits from the Boston chapter of the tong. My grandpa was the head of the Detroit chapter, making him responsible for hosting out-of-town dignitaries. In their honor, our head chef had cooked up fancy plates not found on the usual menu of our Americanized chop suey joint, including crunchy, succulent gai lan and fishy, salt-infused hom yu.

Though we were past our posted closing time of 11 p.m., the dinner was still going strong. Dad, the consummate host and waiter, dressed in his red uniform, would never kick diners out, no matter how long they took to finish that last bite.

The gathering was actually serious business. A mini crime wave had hit the Chinese restaurants in our area. Owners were being held at gunpoint and robbed of all their day's cash. Leaders from the tong's more established chapters around the country had been streaming into town to make sure my grandpa and his friends had things under control. The long faces of our guests suggested they had their doubts.

Close to midnight, as the old Chinese men kvetched and plotted, four young white men dressed in tight T-shirts and even tighter jeans tapped at our big glass window. Surprised to see our lights still on, their faces broke out in smiles.

Even at age 12 my gaydar was fully operational; it was pinging like a busted car alarm. Before I could even make the case to turn the men away so we could wrap up for the night without any awkward clashes, my dad opened the door and issued his signature hearty greeting: "Welcome to Chung's!"

The new arrivals sat down and scanned our menu, but they kept leaning over and staring at the foods spinning on the lazy Susan at my grandpa's table. My dad explained that those dishes weren't on the menu—and as the restaurant was technically closed, the cooks would only be able to make something quick and easy. The men accepted the restrictions with grace. Our cooks whipped up a few of our most popular dishes: savory plates of shrimp fried rice and chicken chop suey. As usual, the staff made a little extra for us kids, along with plates for my grandpa and his guests.

But when my dad, the super host, went to serve the quartet, he surprised them. "It turns out we had a little extra," he said, setting down free samples of the off-menu dishes.

Peering over from the back table, by the coatrack and high chairs, I felt super nervous. Even as an American-born Chinese kid, *I* didn't like some of those pungent dishes. How would these white guys respond?

With cautious forks and spoons in hand, they looked around their party, wondering who would make the first move. The guy with the tank top and biceps who seemed to be the leader nodded before conducting a quick smell-and-taste test.

One small nibble led to another. Soon they were scarfing everything down like Jabba the Hutt.

When my dad went to clear their plates, they joked, "Where can we get these recipes?"

My dad winked. "I guess you'll just have to come again."

As the young men headed out, laughing, they swung by the table of old Chinese men. The gay guys prattled on about how much they liked these new and unfamiliar dishes, pointing at their favorite entrées on the table. And the old guys smiled.

After the foursome left, the members of the tong seemed to lighten up a bit, leaning back in their chairs and taking swigs of their Hennessy. It looked as if they were relishing their food even more than before, as if they took pride in the compliments. At that point I realized I'd been holding my breath through the entire encounter.

Perhaps I shouldn't have been so scared. The Chinese and gay communities shared something in common: In a union town full of Midwestern nuclear families, both groups were outliers. After being marginalized, attacked, and, in some instances, murdered, each had developed their own support system. Each community had learned how to take care of themselves. Was it so much of a stretch that they could take care of each other too?

I had an equal desire to sit at both tables. Back then, even though I knew I was gay and Asian, I didn't think anyone else fit that profile. I thought I had to choose. But seeing how the two groups of men were able to connect, albeit briefly, gave me hope that these two sides of myself might just be compatible.

It could have been coincidence, or something I hadn't noticed before, but after that night it seemed like our gay customers started dining in more, as opposed to ordering takeout. My dad started having longer conversations with them about developments in the neighborhood, including the latest real estate deals and crime reports. Eventually, my dad and some of our gay customers even set up an informal neighborhood watch—although that's a story for another time. This one is about how, thanks to a few shared plates of gai lan and hom yu, our table got a little bigger.

DAVID STREITFELD

Time Is Strong

FROM *Slow Reader*

LONG AGO, IN my vulnerable youth, MFK Fisher gave me some advice.

She was talking about the great love of her life, Dillwyn Parrish. As all Fisher fans know, she met Tim, as he was called, when she was married to Al, the kind of guy who would rather teach romantic poetry than live it. After Fisher got a good look at Tim, Al was done. But in those days, proper young Whittier women did not get divorced because they were smouldering with passion. So Tim and Al and Mary Frances all lived together, setting up housekeeping on the hills above Lake Geneva. Briefly.

Telling me about it a half-century later, Fisher shook her head. "These menages a trois," she said. "They never work out."

Fisher's advice tended to take the form of observations but were delivered in a tone that made it clear you ignored them at your peril. One day, I saw Fisher when I was on my way to one of the spas that populate the wine country. She was dubious at my plans to engage in the popular practice of immersing myself in volcanic ash.

"I don't think I'd want to lie around in someone else's mud," she said.

It was 30 years before I could take another mud bath.

When Fisher was not instructing, she was effortlessly keeping me off-balance. On one visit I was accompanied by my friend Ronnie, another admirer who, unlike me, was an excellent cook. We told Fisher we would bring her lunch. Hours went into dreaming up dishes that would please the woman who had done so much to link sensuality and eating.

We arrived, hampers in hand. "I've made you lunch," Fisher immediately announced. But look, we said, we brought you lunch, just like we said we would. This gave us a dilemma: eat what Fisher had prepared and know we would become an anecdote about how fans not only took up her time but demanded to be fed as well, or serve our repast and turn into a different story about rude fans who spurned the lunch she had painstakingly made for them with her arthritic hands. There was no solution but to eat everything.

Ronnie had made a fruit vinaigrette that did excellent things to a bowl of strawberries and blackberries. "Is there honey in it?" Fisher asked, tasting it. "Honey and lemon juice? It's a simple idea, kind of fun. I like it. But I like the berries better without." And she pushed the vinaigrette to the side, rather forcefully.

This was the Fisher credo: Eat what you want, when you want, the way you want, and make no apologies.

Her second husband, Donald Friede, once noted that Mary Frances "feels that breakfast is not so much a meal as a preamble to the day ahead. On this very sound theory she may drink a glass of vermouth and eat a toasted muffin, or she may decide that what she wants is a plate of hot buttered zucchini. I have seen her start the day with a cold leg of Mallard duck, carefully set aside the previous evening for that particular purpose, and a glass of wine."

It's easy to admire this independence from conventional thought, harder perhaps to live with it, hardest of all to actually practice it yourself. But maybe I should have heeded this advice too. The first time I visited Fisher I was supposedly there to do an interview, not get schooled in life, but my motivations were secretly complicated. I was a young idiot, madly in love with a woman I could not be with. She was a serious Fisher buff. Interviewing Fisher, then, was a substitute, a gift, a mission to prove I was worthy. Except I wasn't worthy. For one thing, I hadn't read nearly enough of her works before plunging headlong into the project, and my ignorance showed.

Fisher was warm and then cold and then warm again, proclaiming her utter disregard for her own work while showing off entire closets stuffed with reprints, telling saucy tales of her past but bridling at questions, inviting us back even as she was kicking us out. She was both too close and too distant for me to see clearly, a woman who used her beauty to make it in a male world at a real cost to her spirit, a writer who had never sold—"All my books were duds"—who was nevertheless an icon, a person who seemed so self-assured but was prone, we know now, to debilitating depression. I could never capture her. I couldn't even keep up my end of the conversation.

She, on the other hand, had no trouble sizing me up.

"You're not negative," she said. She looked at me intently for a moment, which was all it took to make a diagnosis. "You're just morbidly pessimistic. You're an old neurotic." She also called me lugubrious, which I have to admit nailed me pretty well.

I never wrote the article, never even seriously tried, although my beloved prepared a book-length transcript from the tapes. I recently pulled out my Fisher box and read the conversations for the first time. Immediately, I was thrust back to Fisher's bedroom in the little white house that her friend and patron, David Pleydell-Bouverie, had built for her on his Sonoma estate.

You arrived by driving up a lane that relied on signs to keep people out: "Cross fire rifle range," a standard California ranch sign, and "Violators will be prosecuted." Fisher said that Herb Caen, the San Francisco newspaper columnist and wit, suggested adding, "Tropical Disease Experimental Station."

She was having a buzzer installed, to ring if she fell or felt ill. "I'm in a buzzable stage," she said. She tried to make the best of her failing powers. "Edith Sitwell says that every self-respecting woman should spend one day a week in bed. Pretty tough to do that and earn a living. I dislocated my hip twice in six weeks. I'm not bedridden but houseboundish."

The transcript has many squirm-inducing moments I will not share but there are some comments worth preserving that show the writer creating her own mythology as easily as breathing. Some were the anecdotes she told over and over despite their unbeliev-ability, like the one about how the editors of her first book expected MFK Fisher to be a man. But even with the chestnuts her voice came through, soft and urgent as a caress:

> I began to cook when I was five or six, on the cook's day out. It's an ego trip, a wonderful way of getting attention. And I loved getting attention, because my younger sister was sickly. I didn't take attention away from her, I never had any ambition to do that, I just liked to get it too. I learned very early on to make sponge cake, which Father always thought was beautiful.

Just beyond her house, there was a tower with a bell:

> David won that for thirty-seven bucks from Old Man Hearst.
> A while ago, one of his sons, I think it was William Randolph
> Junior, asked David to buy it back. They offered him 3,600
> bucks, or 3,700, whatever it was. David said, "Not on your life.
> We have a tower. Why have a tower with no bell?" And he's not
> going to get another bell. Old Man Hearst, when he wanted
> a bell, he just raped ten monasteries and got twelve bells. . . .
> It's from San Simeon. It has a beautiful tone, too. We ring it
> every night at twilight.

Her novel, *Not Now but NOW*, first issued in 1947, had recently
been reissued by North Point Press. It begins in a very Fisheresque
way: "The nearest Jennie ever came to being untrue to Jennie was
the night all four of them were staying with her." As she wrote in a
new afterword: "Of course I had to borrow from my own life, since
I do not often remember any other."

"I think some people have one novel in them, some people
have a lot more—and some people shouldn't have any," she said.
"I got conned into writing a novel once. Pat Covici, my editor, and
my husband Donald, who was my agent, they both said, 'Write a
novel.' Pat said, 'Every person has to write one novel,' and Donald
said, 'You write a novel and it's going to be a bestseller, and I'll
sell it to Hollywood.' And neither was right. All three of us were
wrong. Because it was never a novel. It was called a novel."

In truth, by the time she wrote *Not Now* she had written one novel
with Tim, published under a pseudonym, and one about Tim that
was issued posthumously. But acknowledging those books would
have hurt her argument that she was an innocent lured into fiction.

"I'd call *Not Now* a cheap lowdown literary trick," she said. "It's like
five novels put together with a time trick. And it sold like peanuts,
it sold like nothing at all. It got critically esteemed because it was
pretty well written. It's kind of like hammock stuff, I think."

In any case, she had moved on from fiction.

"I don't read novels much anymore. Once, I read every novel ever
written. I don't know why I stopped. Why don't I like symphonic
music anymore? It's just a change in taste. Now I like really intricate
chamber music. It's a change. One grows up or grows down."

Donald was a bon vivant, a swashbuckling fellow who, Fisher said, attended Harvard, Yale and Princeton—all in the same year. Working with Covici, he brought out books by Steinbeck, ee cummings, Radclyffe Hall, Albert Einstein, Nathanael West. He rejected an unknown writer's book called *O Lost*, which in Maxwell Perkins' hands became *Look Homeward, Angel.* But Donald couldn't replace Tim, no one could.

"He was more trouble than the children!" Fisher said. "I had to borrow some money once, and when Father found out it was to pay Donald's wife's alimony he almost disowned me he was so furious."

Donald's obituary in the *New York Times* in 1965 gave him his due—"He knew what was going on in a writer's mind and heart," said Pulitzer-winning novelist MacKinley Kantor—but did not mention Fisher at all. "I don't care," she said. Donald was a few years older than Fisher but Tim was fourteen years her senior. That helped. "I like older men. They have more experience and they teach me things." And then she said, even more softly, perhaps to herself: "I teach them things too."

Her parents, Rex and Edith, come off as rather formal in her books but she recalled their wild years:

> After they got married my parents both turned into what we would now call hippie dropouts from society, and my father became a beachcomber for two years. We lived in a house way up on Puget Sound. The Japanese freighters used to come in with rafts of rare woods, like teak and mahogany. Father would row out, and if a log broke off—he didn't break any off, but if a log broke off and it was going to shore, he got it and he sold it to cabinet makers. Money got thin so they came down to Southern California. I was three when Father was a beachcomber. And mother stood it, I don't know how. Because she was very conservative—not a frightened person at all, but socially not very daring. Father went to Ventura and took an option on an orange grove. The day before the option was to come due he thought how strange, the trees are not growing at all. And he dug down and it was hardpan. No hope for the trees at all. So he raced to the town, got his option back—that five thousand bucks was all they had left in the world. And of course within a year that land was sold for oil. My family used to get a bottle of white wine and talk about it. "Isn't it awful? What would have happened if we turned into millionaires? It would be ghastly." We'd say, "Thank God we're not rich." None of us liked money very much.

Fame was a topic she didn't like. She might give advice but liked to think of herself as a neglected voice:

> I don't think I've had very much influence except when the kids were bringing home their friends from school. They would say, "Oh, Mrs Fisher this tastes so fresh." I found out people don't really eat much fresh food. They're always eating frozen pizzas. I know a woman, a very fine sensitive person, who has lived for forty-seven years in the Napa Valley and doesn't know one end of a wine bottle from the other.

She didn't care about recognition, she always said, but she did:

> I was maybe thirty-five and I'd published three or four books. At the table I said, "Rex, did you ever get that autographed copy of my last book?" Nobody had ever mentioned it, you see. They didn't even know I had a last book. And he looked very strangely at me and said, "Yes, I did read it." Not, "It was good." Or "It was terrible" or "It stinks" or anything. So I banged both my hands on the table and said, "Goddamnit, you'd think that every time I publish a book it's as if I had tertiary syphilis." I burst into tears, which I had never done at home before, and stalked from the room.

Fisher was one of those writers—James Salter is another—who teach you how to live, whether you consciously realize it or not. "I saw food as something beautiful to be shared with people instead of as a thrice-daily necessity." This was advice for everyone.

As I've gotten older, I've finally read just about everything by Fisher and many of those in her circle, even Tim's rather forgettable novels. She's a classic now, although I doubt she'll ever have the mass appeal of, say, Anthony Bourdain. She would have said she didn't want it anyway.

The piece that I return to most often, that has the deepest lessons and the most echoes not only for thinking about Mary Frances but for my own life, is "The Standing and the Waiting," collected in *Serve It Forth*. It is about returning to a prized Dijon restaurant after six years, this time with Tim instead of Al; requesting a favorite waiter, Charles, who does not live up to his reputation and spills everything; and finding out, after the meal is ended and

Charles has left, that he had been fired earlier that day and this was his last meal.

It's not simply a story about the passing of time but something harder and more complex, almost cruel. Early in the meal, Tim says, "Time is strong." Fisher laughs at him. "I'm not afraid of time," she replies. But she learns over the course of the evening to at least respect it, to be aware of the way it gives and takes, often simultaneously. Fisher worries the restaurant will not live up to her memories, but it does; Charles, an alcoholic, recovers from his initial clumsiness to do an excellent job of serving. When the couple asks for good marc, a potent digestif, Charles brings them the finest bottle from the cellar and insists they drink nearly all of it. It is too much of a good thing and comes close to ruining the evening. A little taste would have been better. Is Charles trying to reward the couple for being happy in love, or to punish them? Perhaps he is merely taking revenge on the restaurant by giving away one of its oldest and best bottles.

As Mary Frances and Tim leave, the proprietor gives a Gallic shrug about poor Charles. "It was sad—a fine waiter once, a brave little man always—but what will you do?" he says. "Everything changes. Everything passes." Charles is all of us.

While writing this, I went up to the wine country for a weekend. From the highway, I gazed at Fisher's last house, still standing in the middle of its field, a miraculous survivor of the devastating Nun's Fire in 2017. The little cafe at the edge of the highway where we used to have breakfast was gone. Sonoma was less hangdog, more wealthy. I took my first mud bath in decades. I didn't like it much. Somewhere the ghost of MFK Fisher was shaking her head.

Foraging New York City's Wild, Edible Margins with Journei Bimwala

FROM *Grist*

JOURNEI BIMWALA IS quick to spot the yellow, trumpetlike blooms in a meadow of mostly blue vervain, goldenrod, and mugwort along the western bank of the Bronx River. As she forages, she often scans her environment for unusual colors or breaks in familiar patterns, and she recognizes the newcomers as daffodils. She'd never seen them on this seven-acre corridor of land called Concrete Plant Park, one of just two city parks where foraging is allowed. Yet she isn't surprised. "Wild plants move around, like people," she says. "They're very nomadic."

These quiet changes in the landscape delight Bimwala, who gathers much of what she eats from green spaces like this one in New York City, tucked between a subway line and a highway. Foraging awakens a "childlike curiosity" to understand the overlooked wild foods and medicines there for the taking by anyone with a discerning eye. Of course, developing the expertise to see them takes patience, skill, and a willingness to heed nature's cues. "It's not just the ability to recognize a plant, identify it, and take it," Bimwala says. "You actually have to build a relationship with your environment."

Bimwala forages daily, relying on the city's edible margins to provide about 25 percent of what she eats and all of her medicine. Her pantry teems with fruits like persimmons, plums, and crab apples; greens like dandelion, chickweed, and purple dead nettle; and tinctures and salves made from pine pollen, elderberry, and witch hazel. "My whole house is overtaken by earth," she says. Sometimes she forages simply for pleasure, clipping a flower early so she can observe "the whole budding-to-blooming in my house."

Simply put, foraging is the act of identifying and gathering herbs, plants, mushrooms, berries, and other edibles. Although most often considered something done in a forest or meadow or other stereotypically "natural" locations, a growing number of people are taking up the activity in urban locales. It takes time to learn a landscape's flora, a necessary prerequisite for foraging safely and environmentally, but many who embrace the practice find the benefits—including improved mental health and food security—well worth the effort.

For Bimwala, this practice provides fresh ingredients, from elderberry to sumac to wild chamomile, that otherwise can be costly or hard to find. No matter her economic circumstances or the state of the world, she can always rely on the local environment to help provide for her physical and mental well-being. A few hours foraging, using nothing more than scissors to harvest her bounty and a paper bag to carry it, always lifts her spirits. But nature can be a strict teacher. One lesson she's learned: Miss the window of something blooming or fruiting, and she's out of luck until next year. "The plants are teaching me not to be tardy," she says.

It's this emotional and physical connection to the natural world, often lost when living in a big city, that draws many people to foraging. "Sure, getting some free food out of a vacant lot is cute, but it's a much deeper and more spiritual practice," says Candace Thompson, who manages Stuyvesant Cove Park, the only other city park where foraging is allowed. They also explore foraging as a practice through their media project The Collaborative Urban Resilience Banquet. "Even on a shitty Bushwick sidewalk, [you can] look around at the way the seasons change," Thompson says. They especially like to observe which wild plants bloom and how they differ from the previous year. "It has just opened up a whole new way of paying attention," they say.

Throughout the pandemic, amid supply chain disruptions and collective unrest, Bimwala and fellow foragers have spent ever more time immersed in the activity. She encourages others to embrace the practice, hosting classes and individualized mentorship in foraging and herbalism. In that sense, she is teaching people to rely on themselves, and the Earth. "When everything goes wrong, nature is always around," she said. "Nature is your fallback."

Getting to Know the Edible World

Bimwala's foraging journey began seven years ago when she was walking in Pelham Bay Park in the Bronx. She spotted a leafy green plant with soft-white hairs and a "beautiful, very distinguished scent," and immediately had to know more. Bimwala snapped a photo and tumbled down a "Google rabbit hole" that led her to its name: mugwort.

Bimwala now considers mugwort—an abundant perennial with medicinal properties—her "first plant." Whenever she encounters an unfamiliar plant, she relies on a similar process of snapping a photo and turning to the internet for help identifying it. The process can be slow, like learning a new language, but regional foraging guides, engaging online educational content from foragers like Alexis Nikole Nelson and Gordon Walker, and cookbooks like Marie Viljoen's *Forage, Harvest, Feast* make things a bit easier.

After identifying the plant, Bimwala is careful to listen to her body, which helps her understand how to use it. "I start to document my own experience with the plant, so I will taste it in tea. I will taste it in a tincture. I will taste it in food and different variations, seeing how my body feels about the plant and how I'm reacting to it," she says. Like foraging, it's a process that requires a degree of trust in her senses, a skill that develops over time.

A location like the Bronx River Foodway in Concrete Plant Park is a good one to start foraging—a place where the practice is legal, none of the plants are sprayed with chemicals, and the soil is tested for residual pollutants. Online resources like Falling Fruit—a crowdsourced map of more than half a million foraging spots worldwide—and apps like Forager Diary or Wild Edibles can lead beginners and old hands alike to fruitful locations. Bimwala gives tours of the foodway, teaching people to identify plants, pick just what they need, and exercise caution, like testing the soil and learning the land's history.

She leads me along a similar tour, beginning with a rose bush, its buds still tight like fists. "So many parts of the rose are edible," muses Bimwala. For now, she'll pick a few buds to distill as a tincture; later, she may gather the petals, careful to leave the buds so they can emerge as rose hips. "You have to be considerate of the plant's cycle," she says. "I'm not taking everything, killing the plant, and putting animals at risk of losing some of their nutrition." Like a considerate housemate, she always leaves some of the plant for others.

Near the rose bush is an elder bush just beginning to reveal buds. Bimwala tends to gather them sparingly, leaving some to ripen into elderberries, a fruit that is popular (and pricey) because of its antioxidant qualities. A key to identifying the sought-after plant is looking for raised knobs along its smooth gray-brown bark. "If you touch [the bark], you can feel it," says Bimwala. "If it doesn't have it, then it is not elder." She takes other precautions to avoid poison and contamination, like not picking close to the pathway, where animals urinate. Fruits with exterior skin, higher off the ground in a tree, tend to be the lowest risk.

Just beneath the elder bush, creeping plants spread out like a soft green blanket. "This is chickweed," says Bimwala, pointing to its smooth, egg-shaped leaves. "Another one that I have to forage on the constant. It's really a great edible. You can steam it, and you can eat it raw on a salad." The chickweed is growing alongside cleavers, with straggling, sticky stems. Another favorite, she gathers it daily to blend into smoothies with cucumber, lemon, and ginger.

As we walk, we are greeted by wild patches of purple dead nettle's low-hanging, fuzzy green leaves with purple tops and pink flowers. Bimwala encourages me to take handfuls because there is plenty of this so-called invasive weed, which she dries into a tea, to go around.

Bimwala doesn't use the words *invasive* or *native*, a binary rooted in harmful human categories. She notes how some people consider dandelion an invasive weed when it appears in a lawn, but others happily buy dandelion root tea in health food stores. Many other so-called invasives, like chickweed and mugwort, are dense with nutritious and medicinal benefits—if more people only knew how to look for them.

Reclaiming a Suppressed Practice
As a best practice, Bimwala and other foragers are careful not to over-pick a plant that is scarce, but tend to not shy away from harvesting what is abundant. By understanding an ecosystem's needs,

foragers can act as stewards. As Thompson puts it, "We could be eating our ecosystem back into balance as a community," an approach that requires foraging with biodiversity in mind. For instance, they point to how wild ramps have surged in popularity, harvested recklessly to a point of scarcity.

As an alternative, they recommend field garlic, also known as onion grass, loathed by some gardeners who consider it a stubborn weed. But Thompson says it's a delicious, versatile food that works beautifully in pesto or *pajeon*, Korean pancakes typically made with scallions. It can also be infused in vinegar or oil, and the bulbs can be dried into an onion powder. "If you break the hollow stem and it smells like onions, it's edible," says Thompson. (If it doesn't smell like onions, stay clear.) Once you become familiar with it, you'll find field garlic everywhere.

Although every culture has a history of foraging and the practice was once commonplace throughout the United States, it remains illegal across broad swaths of the country, amid mounting pressure to change that. Many of these prohibitions date to emancipation, when anti-foraging laws targeted recently freed Black people, limiting their opportunities for self-sufficiency and economic independence. This differs from, say, Scotland, where a "right to roam" law gives people the right to forage, even on some portions of private property, for personal consumption.

For many foragers, this history makes their practice inherently political, a way of pushing against prohibitive, racist laws that continue to, as Thompson says, "strip people of their ability to find food for themselves outside of the capitalist system." It's this stepping outside of extractive economies that also draws Mo Wilde to the practice, which she refers to in her forthcoming book as "one of the last wild acts of defiance against the concrete world," given that it doesn't require a degree or money—just training one's senses.

And for now, foraging largely remains an act of defiance against the law, too. Foragers would like to see the practice legalized and integrated into city parks. For instance, Bimwala points to how foragers could help public spaces by foraging plants typically managed by chemical sprays or weeding. She sees Concrete Plant Park's food forest as a "testing ground" to show other cities how to design beautiful, edible parks, packed with food and medicine for those ready to learn the land.

But Bimwala also doesn't want people to get so comfortable with food forests, like the bountiful corridor of the Bronx, that they begin to think of uncultivated nature as something to avoid. "Why are we making nature such a scary thing?" she asks. After all, with just a little time and diligence, anyone can see the world differently—and learn to spot wild yellow blooms in a familiar meadow.

He Knew It All

FROM *Grub Street*

ON JULY 15, 1978, Alain Sailhac reported for his first shift as the new chef at Le Cirque, which had been closed for summer break. Except for the butcher and a lone saucier, the entire kitchen staff had walked out with the previous chef. Sailhac spent the next 15 days recruiting a brigade of two dozen cooks. On the restaurant's reopening, Le Cirque owner Sirio Maccioni assured Sailhac that he planned to run the dining room way below capacity. Instead, the 92-seat restaurant did 190 covers for dinner. It was the start of an eight-year run that advanced Le Cirque toward an assured place in restaurant history and put Sailhac on a course to transform food culture in New York.

"He was already changing the stereotype of the classic French restaurant, which was stuck in the '60s and '70s," says Daniel Boulud, the chef who took over Le Cirque's kitchen from Sailhac in 1986. Sailhac was 42 when he landed at Le Cirque, and he immediately settled into a rhythm: 600 covers per day, six days a week, offering a preposterously large menu with an additional eight to ten daily specials.

At one time, he was poised for superstardom, but Sailhac, who died at home in New York City on November 28 after a long illness, never ascended to the celebrity heights of his contemporaries. Instead, friends and those who worked with him see Sailhac's legacy as a chef and craftsman who possessed a unique flair for nurturing talent. In a career that spanned half a century, he trained hundreds of cooks—Geoffrey Zakarian, Terrance Brennan, David Bouley, and Michael Lomonaco among them.

"I always thought Alain was a poet—I don't think he cared to be an entrepreneur," Boulud says. "He was a good mentor and a good man who took good care of his people in the kitchen."

Sailhac was born in Millau, France, in 1936. During the German occupation of France, the six Sailhac children survived on black bread, which often was rationed out by troops with a thick shell of mold. Alain's mother trimmed the loaves and served them with lung, the cheapest offal the family could find, simmered in béchamel. At one point, his older brother spent six months in prison for stealing gasoline from the Nazis.

At a family wedding, a 14-year-old Sailhac encountered a chef who had stories of cooking in exotic places like New York and Singapore. When Sailhac told his father, a glove manufacturer, that he wanted to be a cuisinier, his father said that only women cook. He eventually changed his mind and arranged an apprenticeship for his son at a friend's restaurant, which had a Michelin star.

In 1965, after stints in Guadeloupe and on cruise ships, Sailhac moved to New York to work at Le Mistral and Le Manoir. He was among the first chefs to receive four stars from the *New York Times*—at Le Cygne. "This is a restaurant where even the simplest, most mundane menu selection gets superior treatment," wrote Mimi Sheraton in 1977. Even then, Sailhac was keyed into the quality that would become his trademark.

In fact, Sailhac was confused to learn that the *Times* was coming to take his photo at all. He thought star counts for restaurants stopped at three as with Michelin. "I didn't know what that meant, because I didn't read the paper," he said. Nevertheless, the glory was short-lived: Ten weeks after the review, the owners told him they'd found someone who could do his job for a fraction of the pay.

Sailhac went back to France, where he planned to stay, until his friend André Soltner called. Soltner—who bought the famed Lutèce from Andre Surmain in 1972 and famously missed only a handful of services over the course of 40 years—had once walked into the kitchen at Le Mistral to meet Sailhac after sensing an immediate connection through his food. Now, over the phone, Soltner told Sailhac he had "something interesting" and to expect a letter from Maccioni.

At the time, Le Cirque had some culinary credibility—famous

for its spaghetti alla primavera, for which Maccioni took credit while nodding to his former chef and the artist Edward Giobbi— but it was mostly a place where self-appointed VIPs and bona fide power brokers collided over what must have seemed like perfectly fine carpaccio. After all, this was the dining room where Richard Nixon perpetually outlined his comeback plan over stuffed Dover sole, exiled royal families siphoned inlays of caviar out of ice blocks, and A-list actors swooned over lobster salad.

Shortly into the Sailhac era, however, Maccioni quadrupled the truffle budget and reluctantly built a pastry kitchen, which served crème brûlée that was so ultralight that no fewer than *six maîtres de cuisine* flew in from France to learn the secrets of this dessert.

Geoffrey Zakarian, the chef and future Food Network fixture, was in the kitchen as well. "I'd worked around the corner at Quo Vadis for a couple of months, but I had heard through the grapevine that Le Cirque was where you wanted to be," he says. "I initially walked in without an appointment and asked Alain for a job. I even offered to work as an apprentice just to learn, and it worked."

Sailhac, who enjoyed biking to work, was suddenly able to source all the ingredients he'd ever read about and wanted to cook: Hawaiian blue prawns, New Zealand gooseberries, samphire from coastal France, cèpes from Italy, and scallops in the shell with the roe still attached from Maine—sometimes all on the same day. Those would turn into each evening's specials.

"You just got some marvelous new ingredient you've never worked with," Zakarian recalls, "and Alain would tell you about it and give you one sentence of instruction and walk away."

The pace for cooks on his line was almost impossibly fast, says Charles Dale, who would later become *Food & Wine*'s Best New Chef. Instead of taking the time to read each ticket, they learned to memorize every new order, six orders at a time, or risked losing track of what they were cooking. "I can still hear his voice in the back of my head," Dale says. "It was short and clipped. You didn't really even have time to say, 'Yes, Chef.'"

Michael Lomonaco, a native of Bensonhurst, Brooklyn, says one of the first things he noticed on arriving at Le Cirque in 1986 was that the diversity of kitchen staff "reflected New York in the mid-'80s as I know it," who were joined by veteran French cooks. "One thing I learned from him was this sense to accommodate the guest. If it could be done, it would be done." For example, Sailhac made coulibiac of salmon and off-menu veal kidneys with mustard sauce for guests who requested them. One former cook remembers Sailhac hand-sculpting tiny ducks from clay and filling each with duck confit and a duck egg.

"I never saw Sailhac get flustered by anything that was thrown at him. He knew it all," says David Shack, who worked at Le Cirque from 1982 to 1983. Shack remembers a time in Le Cirque's basement with Sailhac "in a rain slicker, wielding a chainsaw on a huge block of ice to make a sculpture that a party had requested," he says. "Hard to imagine a chef today with that ability."

Sailhac developed a reputation as a cook's cook—so much so that he was able to draw the most famous European chefs across the ocean. Paul Bocuse made repeat visits and was stunned by Sailhac's lamb *champvallon*—an obscure, literal meat-and-potatoes dish from the 1800s. One night at Maccioni's apartment, Sailhac folded perfect *tournée* potatoes and carrots into a bollito misto of tongue and brisket for a freshly landed delegation that included Bocuse, Jacques Maximin, Alain Chapel, and Roger Vergé. (Pastry chef Gaston Lenôtre was supposed to attend, but his plane was stuck circling the airport.)

Eventually, Sailhac needed a break. Unfortunately, his next gig was at 21. His co-chef was a former anthropologist and wunderkind named Anne Rosenzweig, and the *Times* described the duo as "sort of like pairing Madonna and Yves Montand in a musical." They were walking into a mess. The restaurant had recently changed hands. Sailhac fired 23 line cooks and hired 39 replacements. While former FOH staffers set up a picket line on West 52nd Street, millionaire regulars who had lost their go-to lunch spot during the fracas protested in the pages of the "Style" section of the *Times*. (Eileen Ford: "This thing just has to end fast.") In the kitchen, Sailhac and Rosenzweig did what they could. They replaced the beloved creamed chipped beef with pan-fried sweetbreads with roasted tomatoes and "truffle-freckled" potatoes. They put herb butter on the burger. Business soon crescendoed back up to 800 covers a day.

The third of the three outsize institutions in which Sailhac found himself was the Plaza during the hotel's Donald Trump–owned, *Home Alone 2: Lost in New York* era. Maccioni had connected the chef with Ivana, a Le Cirque regular who demanded he start as culinary director the following day. The Trumps ran the place together while Donald courted tabloids to brag about his impending divorce. (As a stunt, he once posted a pair of armed guards outside Ivana's office to stop her from working.) Sailhac didn't seem to understand the Trumps: "They were very, very generous with me," he said later, "but it became very uncomfortable."

In the early '90s, Sailhac met Arlene Feltman at De Gustibus Cooking School. Lomonaco, who had taken over 21 as chef, said the couple would come in on date nights to order pasta and veal scallopine. "These weren't even on the menu," he says, "but they knew I would make anything for them." The pair soon married and traveled the world.

It was Dorothy Cann Hamilton who first convinced Sailhac to start teaching, in 1999, at the French Culinary Institute (which later became the International Culinary Center and eventually merged with the Institute of Culinary Education). At the FCI, Sailhac crossed paths with a surfeit of talent while they were students—Wylie Dufresne, David Chang, Christina Tosi, Dan Barber, Lee Anne Wong. He formed a French-chef supergroup with Jacques Torres, Jacques Pépin, and André Soltner, who came out of post-Luttèce retirement to teach.

"For me, he was like a brother," Soltner says of their 60-year friendship. "We became friends right away and stayed friends." The two would cook together both at the school and at their summer homes in France (Sailhac's in Menton, Soltner's in Cannes). The two cooked together so many times, Soltner says, that it would be impossible to single out any one meal as the most memorable. "We cooked our whole lives," he says. "Really, our whole lives."

JAYA SAXENA

Is the "Future of Food" the Future We Want?

FROM *Eater*

THE CONFERENCE ROOM at the Bellagio hotel swelled with the horns of "Ride of the Valkyries." On a theater-sized screen set up at the front, I watch as a drone flies over a low, sunny suburb, bypassing highways and beaches and nondescript homes, where in the backyards everyone cranes their necks to see what this spidery black object is zooming across the sky. Finally, the drone reaches its destination—a home much like all the others it passed—and a panel opens on one side to reveal a bag from El Pollo Loco. The bag, held by a grappling hook, lowers to eager customers gazing up like guppies at flakes. Finally it hits a pristine green lawn, where it's picked up by human hands and its contents presumably enjoyed for dinner. "INTRODUCING AIR LOCO FROM EL POLLO LOCO," reads the bright white screen. "THE FIRST NATIONAL RESTAURANT TO DELIVER BY AIR."

"We're here to disrupt the food deliveries industry," says Ben Thein, COO of Flytrex, an Israeli drone delivery company. Partnering with the Mexican grilled chicken chain, the drone system has completed about 500 deliveries so far, mostly in Southern California, with plans to expand in the Dallas area soon. The drones can't deliver to apartments, and can't fly in the rain or in high winds. But if you live in the suburbs within two miles of an ordering location, and the weather is mild and still, you could order food or groceries and it will get to your home in about five minutes, "faster and fresher" than if a human drove it, Thein says. What a bold future.

After a year of hearing about the unstoppable rise of food delivery, I expected a truly wild and alien vision of the future to be presented at the Food On Demand conference in Las Vegas, a convergence of various food-service delivery, production, and mobile ordering companies—delivery robots bumping into my legs, self-driving vans filled with pizza freshly baked en route, maybe that noodle vendor from the *Fifth Element* hovering outside my hotel window. These conversations, after all, were happening within the halls of exxxcess: past the glass Chihuly blossoms hanging in the lobby of the Bellagio, past the extravagant autumnal display of mushroom and dragonfly sculptures towering overhead in the hotel's conservatory and botanical gardens, past the all-Christmas store and the chocolate fountain in the bakery, away from the caviar bar and the casino and the wedding chapel and the tourists with foot-long daiquiris and the famous dancing fountain and the life.

In the windowless beige back rooms, a hundred men (it was vastly men) championed their data collection and organization apps. They asked seemingly easy questions: Why shouldn't you be able to order not just food, but flowers, toiletries, and shoes? Why should geography determine what restaurants you can order from? Why should you ever have to leave the house? Andy Rebhun, SVP digital and marketing officer for El Pollo Loco, noted during the drone demo that "I really don't feel like customers should have to travel to pick up their food." And I sat, watching the drone video and dudes exchanging business cards while making small talk, thinking, *oh fuck* and *is that it?*

Is the American dream never having to go outside? I thought of this in the long walk through the Bellagio back to my hotel room, which distorted my sense of just where the hell I was; signs led the way to corridors and trams to other hotels, with other restaurants, bars, and casinos I could enjoy without ever having to step onto a street.

I did go outside, because it is one of the great joys of being alive to experience a place you've never seen before. I watched the Bellagio fountain show and pretended that pocketing the bathroom lotion counted as my Ocean's 1. I wandered to the Cosmopolitan, and promptly lost $20 on a *Mad Max: Fury Road*–themed slot machine in 45 seconds. I waved hi to feathered showgirls, and as the sun set and the fake Eiffel Tower lit up, I felt earnestly dazzled by this city in the middle of a desert—*holy shit, look at the ridiculous things humans can build.*

But everywhere I looked in Vegas, I saw something I had already seen. I ate one meal at Sadelle's, a restaurant from Major Food Group whose first location is in New York's Soho. To get to my room from there, I passed a JuicePress, which also originated in New York. On the other side of the hotel were Spago and Le Cirque, across the street was some property by Gordon Ramsay, and of course somewhere nearby was a Starbucks. For dinner on my first night, I ate at Night + Market, a Thai restaurant from LA. The next night, I was at the counter at Momofuku, a restaurant whose first location was half a block from my childhood home.

The point that so many attendees of the Food On Demand conference made was that Momofuku should not just exist in New York. In fact, according to Michael Beacham, president of kitchen business for REEF, a company that allows restaurants to expand using ghost kitchens, sticking with solely physical locations— rooms of warmth and design where friends gather, third spaces that anchor communities—is a limited view of what a restaurant can really be: Everywhere at once. He offers, for example, TGI Fridays, a casual chain that has national recognition but little presence in densely populated American cities. "When you have that level of customer affinity, but you're not able to get close enough to them to serve them, you're missing a lot of opportunities," he said. REEF is one of the largest companies (including C3, Virtual Dining Concepts, the Travis Kalanick–backed CloudKitchens, and even DoorDash) to enter the virtual restaurant space in the past few years.

Virtual restaurants technically allow anyone to create and expand a restaurant brand without the costs and hassles of a restaurant location. REEF essentially works as a franchisee by setting up chefs cooking a brand's food (could be a small restaurant just getting started, could be Wendy's) in mobile kitchens in parking lots and on street corners, as well as in the kitchens of other restaurants. That way, restaurants can grow their delivery footprints without opening up new physical locations—or having one at all. "REEF brings the world to the block," says Beacham.

Walking out at the Bellagio, looking across the fountains at the faux Eiffel Tower sitting on top of the Cabo Wabo Cantina, I couldn't think of a better place to sell the concept of everything you want, all the time, immediately. This is what the Food On Demand attendees want to build—celebrity concepts, national brands, and anything you could think to want brought to you with no time to second-guess your choices. If they're bringing the world to the block, the block they're modeling it after is the Vegas strip.

Then they take it a step further: Imagine a world in which your neighborhood, as shown to you on an app, resembles an entirely different neighborhood than the one on your street, where store-fronts have nothing to do with what's available for you to eat. "Eventually the word 'virtual' is just going to be dropped," hopes Alex Canter, co-founder of the virtual restaurant platform Nextbite. "It'll just be restaurants that live online the same way that when you shop online for clothes, you don't call it a 'virtual store.'" The draw of a virtual restaurant is that of online shopping: The same products no matter where you are, or sometimes products exclu-sive to the virtual world. It's fast food on an even grander scale.

However, like the real world, the virtual restaurant world is driven mostly by people who already have a ton of money and influence. The most successful players are established brands, whether it's chains like Popeyes or McDonald's (which is trying to wrest delivery control back from the apps), chefs like Tom Colicchio, or celebrities. "When you look at a celebrity brand, they already have an audience, and you're leveraging that trust that someone has in that celebrity to say, 'I want to try that,'" says Beacham. For instance, REEF partnered with Robert Earl's Virtual Dining Concepts to bring the wildly successful Mr. Beast Burger to international markets, and recently launched a wing concept with DJ Khaled. You can have anything you want, but only if a famous person has approved of it first.

All of this is moot without the power of delivery platforms, how-ever, which are still on the rise. "Pre-pandemic, we had something like 22 million diners, right? Fast forward to April of this year, our last earnings call, we had 33 million," said Kenny Klein, senior director of sales at Grubhub, during a panel on the "big three" delivery apps. That the pandemic "accelerated" delivery's success was the most popular talking point at Food On Demand: "We're never going back to not being able to have what we want, when we want it, and how we want it," REEF's Beacham said. We are emerging in a world in which more people are choosing to order dinner than go grocery shopping, more people have downloaded delivery apps, and more people are willing to try restaurants that only exist online. So of course this brave new world is not about flashy tech; it's about anything that tinkers with the gears that keep the delivery machine running.

If delivery being available to everyone, everywhere, is the future, then restaurants are left to figure out how to not be left in the dust. And of course, the platforms that created this world want to be in on that action. Some of that is by encouraging restaurants to operate virtual restaurants, and some of that is having apps, not chefs or seasonality, guide menu planning ("You don't pare down forever but just pare it down to what makes more sense," Klein said the company has told restaurants).

So here is the future, maybe: You get your Italian subs from Pauly D and your wings from DJ Khaled, or maybe just from a generic brand you've never heard of before, food that's satisfying and unsurprising, things that can be easily executed and delivered to you no matter where you are. In-person restaurants don't die; to experience the avant-garde, the interesting, or anything that doesn't do well sitting in a box for 20 minutes, you need to leave your home. But as the heating and transportation technology gets better, there are fewer experiences that can't be brought right to you. It's so convenient and efficient, the time that you would have spent driving and sitting and waiting for the check can now be spent on . . . well, whatever you want, but work probably. And there's no need to fret when you travel somewhere far from home. You can get the same experience, everywhere, instantly.

This is meant, I think, to make one feel both comfortable and pampered, the overwhelming choice buffered by the safety of familiarity. Yes, you have the world at your fingertips, but you know all the names—it's nothing you haven't heard of before. And while there is novelty and convenience in having the same options in New York or LA or Peoria, Illinois, or Butte, Montana, it also becomes uncanny. The duck ramen at Momofuku inside the Cosmopolitan Las Vegas was as perfectly executed as it could be, but when I exited the restaurant and turned to the right I remembered I was essentially in a mall food court, not a neighborhood. My meal at Night + Market, imported from LA to the Virgin Hotel, was set to the tune of ringing slot machines from the casino floor. These restaurants were here, but not because Vegas offered them anything new: In fact, the strategy behind opening there was exactly the opposite.

The other thing Vegas is trying to sell—outside the concept of Vegas itself—is luck, which as Penn & Teller (err, just Penn) put it the night I saw their show, is "probability taken personally." There is a reason these conventions take place in Vegas, or a reason Vegas built itself to accommodate them—it is easier to spin in your head, among the hospitality and sequins and free drinks, the story of success. That you didn't just happen upon your winnings, but you made them happen with your wit and your choices. The story being spun at Food On Demand was: A world in which everything exists for you to buy in an instant was one we, the consumers, chose. *This is what the people want*, said the men in the bulky sports coats and flimsy lanyards, *and we're just here to give it to them.* Like many stories, you have to wonder how much of it is true.

Conferences are boring and exhausting, and despite being at a food delivery conference in a city built to cater to every whim, many of my food options flat-out sucked. I spent too much on a dry room service omelet stuffed with raw hothouse tomatoes, and a box of coffee for four, which happened to be the smallest size available. A lunch provided by ezCater, a corporate catering company, gave off the whiff of Fyre Festival, with a wilted salad topped with two chickpeas, and a veggie wrap that was soggy and so, so cold. In my whiniest voice, I saw the appeal of everyone's vision: *I'm in Vegas for fuck's sake. Spago should just deliver to my room.*

But a world like that needs to be built, and like the temples and cathedrals and Bellagio fountain, its novelty and impressiveness is meant to distract you from just how it's done. The draw of drone and robot delivery, for instance, is that it saves restaurants from having to pay delivery drivers. "It's about 30 percent cheaper for us right now to do drone delivery versus standard delivery," said Rebhun. "I really don't think, with minimum wages rising, that we're going to be able to continue to do [dispatched driver delivery]." Thein elaborated that "instead of multiple drivers, we can have just one person controlling many drones. This is our way to reduce cost."

Most businesses presented their cost-cutting or logistics-organizing services as a boon, especially to independent restaurant owners who are still struggling due to the pandemic. Saving 30 percent on delivery costs by adding drone delivery is self-evidently positive. In the best-case scenario, this could mean the money saved would be used to pay the remaining workers a higher wage. "I would love to see a more sustainable wage for not just restaurant workers, but for the drivers and everyone involved," said Canter. "The way that there's more to go around is when automation starts to kick in a little bit more than it is today."

It's through a combination of some exploitative labor practices and crafty salesmanship that the idea of cutting labor seems like the natural future for restaurants. During the conference, the ongoing trend of food service workers rethinking jobs that have provided them with low wages and no benefits was euphemistically referred to as things like a "scarcity of drivers," "labor problems," and "cost pressures." And, like with most businesses, workers were mostly framed as a liability rather than an asset. Like, at least Las Vegas is a union town.

At best, drones and apps lead to a sort of fully automated luxury communism, a world in which most labor is automated, leaving humans to leisure and enjoyment. But for that to exist, you need the communism to come before the automation. Apps and auto-mation may create an opportunity for restaurant owners to treat their workers better, but they don't require it. As it stands, without something like a universal basic income, automation becomes a loophole to pay fewer people. It also assumes restaurant owners would use surplus profits to bolster wages for the remaining work-ers, which is a bold assumption. While there is evidence that wages are going up for food service workers, it is largely in response to workers refusing to work for anything less, and restaurant owners acquiescing because they need to stay in business. If a restaurant owner decides to pocket the extra cash and pay their workers a minimum wage that is nothing close to a living wage, that's their choice. The company that lets it deliver food via drone has no skin in that game.

The same goes for virtual restaurants. Every representative from a virtual restaurant company who I spoke to, or who spoke at a panel, was selling how easy it was for owners to implement. Mostly, the work was assumed to be so low-lift that it wouldn't even reg-ister as extra. "Restaurants already have fixed rent. The lights are already on. The staff is already in the kitchen, whether they're doing one brand or multiple brands. So why not do more orders?" asked Canter. "Why not make more food?" But there's nothing stopping a restaurant owner from essentially doubling someone's output without passing on any of the theoretical profits from a robust delivery business. According to workers, that's what's actually been happening.

Fast-food workers recently told Modern Retail that an increase in mobile orders over the past year and a half has them feeling like they're doing two jobs for no extra pay. "Mobile orders in 2021 and 2020 were hell for employees: It was stressful and overworking, and we saw no extra pay for that extra work," said a former Starbucks employee in Toronto. Other workers say that online orders also tend to be bigger than in-person orders, and that the staff on hand is inadequate to handle the volume. "[Corporate's messaging was] you're just doing what you're always doing," said a former McDonald's employee, who left in June. "But it's like, [our work] just quadrupled." At Starbucks, "technology was made for customers and not for employees," one barista told Reuters of the company's mobile ordering app, which frequently inundated a Buffalo location with so many orders they fell 40 minutes behind. And five former Chipotle employees also told Insider they quit after a surge of delivery orders created "impossible" conditions.

This is what happens when a company prioritizes growth and "capturing the market" over the day-to-day reality of the workers. The *Wall Street Journal* reported that REEF has used $1.2 billion in investment to buy up parking lot companies and expand its operations, and is now urgently trying to meet investor expectations. This is all done on the backs of cooks who are expected to work at a breakneck pace, and sometimes in unsafe conditions. Three REEF workers allege being harmed by fireballs erupting from propane burners in a mobile kitchen, with one former market director telling Insider, "our team was deadly afraid to work every day because they thought their face will get burned off." Others said the pressure to send out orders as quickly as possible resulted in lax health regulations, and with customers receiving uncooked or raw food. In a meeting of kitchen division managers, one executive presented a slide that apparently read "Speed: If everything seems under control, you're not going fast enough."

Klein insisted that customers "understand that delivery's a convenience and it is a service," and that we're all, restaurants and customers alike, willing to pay our share for this convenience to exist. But consumers have basically always had their restaurant meals subsidized by poverty wages, and so far, the entire delivery industry has been set up so that the consumers are shielded from how much this convenience truly costs. That disconnect has become more pressing as delivery has become all but a necessity for many restaurants. Restaurant owner Andrew Ding told *Eater's Land of the Giants* podcast that delivery apps have "morphed into . . . basically modern-day mafia," insisting restaurants need them or they'll perish. "I'm not going to say that the platforms don't have a place, because it's a marketplace. It helps for discovery," says Ding, but that's the platforms' argument—the market demands this, we're just here to deliver. Some cities, like Chicago, have gone so far as to sue delivery companies on behalf of restaurant owners and customers alike.

Even if customers understand delivery is a "convenience," apps have regularly fought to erode any remaining friction between desire and satiation, whether it's by keeping gig-worker delivery drivers from unionizing or demanding higher wages, or listing restaurants without their consent so it looks like they have a wider selection. And these men are right—delivery is here and there is no going back.

But if we stay on this trajectory, in which both restaurants and workers are squeezed for the convenience of the customer, and delivery platforms operate on losses in the hopes they'll become a monopoly, it'll look much like every other venture capital–funded "disruption" play that has yet to turn a profit. We've seen how Airbnb's initial pitch of renting out your apartment when you're on vacation has fueled a gentrification and housing crisis. We know that Uber's and Instacart's initial offers of "use your own car to make money in your spare time!" has turned into thousands of people whose wages are reliant on their algorithms. We see that for every independent virtual restaurant brand there are double the amount of celebrity-driven ones churning profit for the already successful, or ghost kitchens just dedicated to making Burger King. And we know that delivery apps like DoorDash and UberEats paid millions to fight legislation that would have allowed drivers to have employment benefits. There is nothing in their Food On Demand pitches that requires a change from how things already are. Like Vegas itself, it's not about creating anything new, just giving you more of it.

*

It is impossible to unhinge the jaw of the ouroboros of desire when it comes to delivery on demand. Did customers already dream of having their 7-Eleven order brought to them from a different ZIP code via an autonomous vehicle, or by someone on an e-bike who basically has to break traffic laws to get it to their door on time, or did they begin dreaming once it was offered? Does it even matter? I admit the immediacy of it all feels off-putting to me in the way walking out on the Vegas strip did, the mistaking of plenty for joy. If every brand becomes a national one, if the only choice I have is between one corporate chain or another, if every meal can be driven or shipped or droned to me from everywhere, if I don't "have to" go anywhere—why be anywhere? Whose problem was that, and did it really need immediate solving?

In some corners, though, we see how different choices can be made. Matt Howard of EatStreet, an independent online delivery service based in Madison, Wisconsin, said the company's drivers are W2 employees and it still manages to be profitable. David Cabello, founder of Black & Mobile, a delivery app that focuses on Black-owned restaurants, spoke about being a "second chance" company, hiring drivers who may have backgrounds that make it difficult for them to be hired elsewhere, and how they focus on treating drivers well. More restaurants continue to experiment with ending tipped wages. Unionization pushes at fast-food restaurants are gaining attention and support. The Buffalo Starbucks location where everyone was burned out on mobile orders? They just unionized.

Having the same means-tested dinner options on every corner (or app) in America does not create value, but neither does scarcity. Opening an app and hiring someone to drive to your house with some burgers and sodas does not have to be an inherently exploitative task. It is pretty objectively a nice thing to have. Using a drone to deliver medicine to people who may live up to 50 miles from the closest pharmacy? Also, in a vacuum, a great idea. What's exploitative is the way it functions: These apps, services, and even restaurants are not built from the standpoint that every worker should be making a living wage on every order. Instead, they're built on the idea that waiting or effort is the same thing as being denied, and on the fact that building a business on the backs of exploited workers isn't considered a fundamentally failed model.

The world these executives are advertising is one of abundance. But by not focusing on the worker, they cannot build this world, and in fact will probably build the opposite of what they claim— a world in which access to takeout dinner from an international slate of virtual restaurants is only available to a few.

Klein is right—building the world of delivery requires consumer education. But squint and you can see it, the actual world of abundance, where drone delivery doesn't have to be traded for lost jobs, where drivers are paid living wages, where line cooks aren't expected to double their output, where consumers understand and pay the true cost of this convenience, where there is a great diversity of offerings from independent businesses, and where everyone can actually afford that convenience both when they need and when they want it. That sort of equity is the actual issue at hand, and what we have the choice to build. Spago arriving at your hotel room door for a mere $2 delivery fee was never the problem that needed solving. The first step is understanding what the real problem is.

JENNIFER FERGESEN

Kimchi with a Side of Whale

FROM *Eater*

JILLIAN MORENO IS cutting maktak—whale skin and blubber—
with an ulu, a curved knife like a handheld half-moon. The maktak
has been in the freezer since the end of the spring whaling season,
and after sitting out for a few minutes it has barely thawed. The
blade passes with the gentle resistance of teeth through an ice
cream sandwich. There's an ice cream note to its appearance,
too—black skin and pink fat as clearly delineated as the chocolate
and strawberry in a tub of Neapolitan.

Moreno slices the maktak into strips the width of her pinky
finger and sprinkles them with salt. "This is how I first had it when
I was a kid," she says, offering me a piece. The skin, smooth and
elastic, smells of the sea—the chill, kelp-steeped breeze of the
Arctic coast of Alaska. The blubber melts against the tongue like
otoro, the fatty belly of bluefin.

"And this is how a lot of people like it these days," she says,
reaching for a plastic tub of kimchi. She spoons some into a bowl,
adds the maktak, and stirs. I try a red-glossed strip, caught against
a sliver of cabbage. The kimchi is fresh, the cabbage crisp as a
cymbal crash against the melting whale. Sesame oil and spice slice
through the fat. It's my first time trying this combination, but being
half Filipino I recognize the equilibrium of salt, fat, acid, and heat—
like fried pork belly dipped in spiced vinegar, sisig tossed with chiles
and calamansi juice.

"I liked it automatically," Moreno says of the first time she tried
maktak with kimchi about 15 years ago. "Maktak is delicious, kimchi
is delicious, and it just works."

Moreno's cross-cultural home—she's Iñupiaq, her husband is Filipino—isn't the only place you'll find maktak and kimchi in Utqiagvik (called Barrow from about 1901 to 2016). On many tables in America's northernmost city, the combination has become as standard as sushi and wasabi. There are tubs of kimchi in many Utqiagvik families' refrigerators and chest freezers, and gallon pails of it regularly arrive from the city to the more remote villages of the North Slope (the surrounding borough) by air freight. Most of this kimchi comes from Sam and Lee's Restaurant, the oldest Asian restaurant in town, but supermarkets have responded to the demand by stocking imported brands, and some home cooks have learned to make their own.

Maktak and kimchi is one of the many hybridizations of niqipiaq (Native foods) that Iñupiat people harvest from the sea and tundra that surround Utqiagvik, a community where a subsistence lifestyle persists despite the supermarkets that now supply barged-in beef, watermelons, and Pop Tarts. The dish is an edible synecdoche for the town, a proudly Iñupiaq place that accepts people and influences from elsewhere with open arms.

If you wish to make maktak and kimchi, you must first kill a whale. The Iñupiat are among the only people in the world who have the legal right to do so. Though commercial whaling is now banned in much of the world (with Japan, Iceland, and Norway notable exceptions), the Iñupiat subsistence hunt is protected under the Marine Mammal Protection Act through a co-management program with the Alaska Eskimo Whaling Commission.

In Alaska, subsistence is a legal term defined by federal law as "the customary and traditional uses by rural Alaska residents of wild, renewable resources" for applications including food, shelter, clothing, and tools. It does not have the connotation of bare-minimum survival that one might read in the dictionary definition, especially for Alaska Natives who now apply this word to the practices that they and their ancestors used to build and support complex, thriving societies.

For a few years in the 1970s, it seemed the Iñupiat would lose their right to their most important subsistence practice. In 1977, the International Whaling Commission banned the subsistence hunt out of concern for declining numbers of bowhead whales. The AEWC formed in response and lobbied the IWC to consider their communities' needs, arguing that they had observed the whale population to be at least twice as large as the census estimated. The IWC allowed a small quota and added acoustic monitoring tools to their census efforts, which revealed that the AEWC was correct—scientists were miscounting whales as they dropped below the ice out of sight of the census station. Today, the North Slope Borough Department of Wildlife Management conducts a regular census of the bowhead whale population, using methods co-developed with the AEWC, to help NOAA and the AEWC set subsistence harvest levels through the IWC. The current strike limit for bowhead whales, set in 2018, is 67 per year.

But against the thousands of years that the Iñupiat and their ancestors have timed to the metronome of the whales' migration, this interruption barely registers. It is effectively an unbroken tradition, sacred and ancient, if augmented now by modern tools like forklifts and snow machines.

In the fall and spring, as bowhead whales swim to and from their summer feeding grounds in the Beaufort Sea, hunters wait for them on the lace collar of ice that frills Utqiagvik's beaches in all seasons but high summer. Iñupiat hunters harvest belugas too, among many other marine and terrestrial animals, but none is as important to the patterns of Utqiagvik life as the agviq (bowhead).

Every successful hunt is an impromptu holiday. After the hunters have taken care of the grueling work of killing and bringing home the whale, more crew members join to help break down the animal. They clamber around the carcass with blades mounted on ax handles, their hands growing slippery and stiff in the blood and cold.

Nearly every part of the whale has a purpose. The blood is collected in bags for mikigaq, a tangy ferment dotted with chunks of meat and fat; the membrane of the liver is saved for a drum skin. The maktak makes up a large portion of the harvest, sliced off the sides in thick, curling slabs like rolls of sod. The flippers and tail are also prime cuts. Some crews pack the maktak in the bottom of an ice cellar, then pile the wine-dark meat on top so that the flavor of the blood permeates the fat.

Whale meat is illegal to sell in most of the United States, but Iñupiat people and other Alaska Natives may sell it within Native towns for Native consumption (with the exception of Cook Inlet beluga, which no one may sell). For the most part, though, maktak is given away freely, and anyone lucky enough to receive this gift may legally consume it.

By the end of every season, the crews give away the bulk of their catch. They divvy up the whales into shares: One might include a generous chunk of maktak, some meat from the body and a piece of tail, plus a cup of boiled fruit cocktail and a fresh-baked roll. Often some of the maktak is boiled, at which point it is called uunaalik. Some shares are distributed soon after the hunt, with the rest set aside for season-end celebrations like Nalukataq in June.

For decades, the town's churches took care of distributing the shares and hosted communal meals in celebration of the harvest. Christianity, especially Presbyterianism, became intertwined with many of Utqiagvik's traditions after a period of assimilationist missionary presence beginning in the 1890s. Sunday attendance has since dropped off, but the churches still serve as community centers, and some host prayer services for the whalers, despite greater recognition of the cultural paternalism that early missionaries brought to the community.

The pandemic prompted the town to adopt a drive-thru format. Last Thanksgiving, a long line of cars tracked through the snow in Simmons Field downtown to receive their shares from the 16 whales killed that season, piled in sacks on frost-covered plastic tables. Every family in town can receive a share, Iñupiat or otherwise, with larger portions for those who assisted the crews in some way during the season.

The share days coincide with an uptick in kimchi sales at Sam and Lee's Restaurant, the source of almost all of the kimchi that is consumed with maktak in and around Utqiagvik. "It sells out so fast when people get their servings," Moreno says. "You have to call ahead if you want it."

Sam and Lee's is a Chinese restaurant at the center of Utqiagvik, where three of its main roads converge. A street sign hung on the barn-red siding reads "Sam N Lee's Pl.," a token of appreciation from the community.

A plastic table bars the entrance to the dining room, closed due to the pandemic. (I visited last July, but as of July 2022 dine-in remains closed.) Owner Louise Kim stands behind it to take orders. Behind her are framed photographs of her four children, some in graduation caps, some in sports uniforms. "Only kimchi is not good for your stomach," she says when I ask for it, and insists on giving me cabbage soup and rice for free. Then she notices that I'm only wearing a denim jacket in the 40-degree summer weather. "Come to my house and I'll give you some warm clothes," she presses.

I politely decline the latter offer, but a few days later I'm sitting in Sam and Lee's dining room as Louise and her husband Hyung Kim cover a table with plate after plate of food. Louise brings me more cabbage soup and rice; Hyung goes into the kitchen to make Mongolian beef scattered with chiles. Then they surprise me with a platter of kimchi and uunaalik they received in the last share. "It's inevitable," says Cynthia, their 23-year-old daughter, when I protest. "They're not going to stop feeding you."

Sam and Lee's has been feeding Utqiagvik Mongolian beef, kung pao chicken, and other American Chinese standards for more than 50 years. Like many small-town Chinese restaurants of its generation, it also serves steaks, burgers, and diner-style breakfast plates of eggs and hash browns. You can get pizza here too, and $40 king crab platters. The only Korean calling card on the menu is kimchi, listed under the salad section, though the restaurant has been Korean-owned for as long as anyone can remember.

Before the Kims took it over, the restaurant was owned by one of Louise's cousins, Chong Park. Park's mother owned another restaurant in Anchorage, where Hyung worked after immigrating to the United States "because of some mishaps in Korea," Cynthia says. On a trip to Hawaii in the late 1970s, the two men met and hit it off so well that Park decided to give Hyung a job at his restaurant. "They also set up kind of an arranged marriage for my mom and dad," Cynthia adds.

Hyung moved to Utqiagvik, then called Barrow, in 1979 to wash dishes at the restaurant. He spoke little English but had no trouble making friends. It helped that he always had food to share, and he was happy to try anything offered to him. He quickly took to Iñupiaq foods such as maktak and credits himself for first combining it with kimchi. "Kimchi has the best taste," he says, explaining that the acidity and spice cloak the slightly fishy scent of the whale. It's the same principle behind Korean dishes like hoe-muchim, a raw fish and vegetable salad coated with gochujang and sesame oil. "I told people to try it, and now everybody eats it," he says.

But if Hyung invented the combination, Louise is likely the one who popularized it. She moved to Alaska in the early 1980s, having met and married Hyung on one of his visits to Korea. They bought the restaurant after her cousin started a new job in Anchorage. Prior to the move, she spent most of her life in a small village in South Korea that she describes as a bucolic place in the mountains, with clean water, fresh vegetables, and neighbors as close as family. "Every time you make some special food, you deliver it to everyone in the village," she says. "In a small village, you help each other." She wanted to do the same in her new home.

In her first years in Alaska, she would show up at every wedding, funeral or birth in town with a stack of containers of food. One would always contain kimchi—not the tart, fermented mugeun-kimchi she makes for herself, but a fresh version she calibrated to local tastes. "I made it mild, not too spicy, a little sweet, a little sour with vinegar, a little sesame oil," she says. She recommended trying the kimchi with maktak, standard fare at Iñupiat family gatherings. Over time, families came to associate the dish with some of the most significant meals of their lives.

Louise still takes food to funerals—"Everybody knows, somebody died, Sam and Lee's coming with food for them," she says—but for celebrations, locals order kimchi themselves. It has become a common craving among pregnant women. Devotees take caches of kimchi with them when they travel, whether they're going on vacation to Hawaii or popping down to Anchorage. A two-week trip might call for a gallon order. "Anchorage is a big city, so there's a lot of Korean food there," Louise says, "but nobody's making kimchi like Sam and Lee's kimchi."

Not everyone in Utqiagvik approves of the kimchi craze. Miranda Rexford-Brown, Ruling Elder of the Utqiagvik Presbyterian Church, remembers the IWC ban and how close her community came to losing their right to hunt. She believes whale should be eaten with moderation and respect, befitting the work that goes into harvesting it—without any adulterants.

"My son, he's 25 years old," she tells me after I visit the church, the oldest one in town, a white-and-green building with its name painted on a bowhead whale scapula outside. "He said he visited a family here, his friends, and they had kimchi from Sam and Lee's Restaurant at the same time they were eating the frozen maktak.

I said, 'That's not the way to eat it! I don't like that, take that away from me!'"

But Jerica Niayuq Leavitt, assistant professor of Iñupiaq Studies at Ilisagvik College in Utqiagvik—the only tribally controlled college in Alaska—says it's possible to prepare niqipiaq in modern ways while still honoring tradition. For the past five years, she's taught a class called Traditional and Contemporary Native Foods Preparation at the college that encourages students to do so. "When you have your Native food, there's a different type of satisfaction," she says. "It feeds your stomach, but it also feeds your soul."

Local hunters, fishers, and foragers provide raw material for the class, including whale, fish, wildfowl, and edible plants like berries and beach greens. After Ilisagvik went remote due to the pandemic two years ago, the class worked from boxes of ingredients—like Blue Apron for niqipiaq—that Leavitt packages and delivers to students' homes. The new model means she can now include students living in distant towns like Anchorage and Nome, who receive their ingredient boxes by air freight. The college has resumed in-person classes, but students still have the option of distance learning.

Students prepare a traditional and a modern recipe for every ingredient. With tuttu (caribou), they've made aluuttagaaq, a rich traditional stew, as well as jerky spiced with hot red chile. When Jillian Moreno took the class, she used her piece of tuttu to make udon soup. "Trying new things with niqipiaq is exciting," Leavitt says. "It's like combining both of our worlds together."

Kimchi is just one of the accompaniments Iñupiat families have come to enjoy with whale in recent years. Several home cooks make a kind of salad with maktak or uunaalik that involves jalapenos, pickles, onion, and pepperoni—checking the same salt, acid, and heat boxes as Sam and Lee's kimchi. Stir-fried uunaalik with vegetables is also popular, as is pickled maktak with carrots and peppers. Many swear by sprinkling maktak and uunaalik with Kunniak's Spices, a line of seasoning blends made by local entrepreneur Kunniak Hopson, instead of the more traditional salt.

Whatever it's paired with, for the people of Utqiagvik, maktak is more than food. "Whaling isn't just a one-day thing, and then you suddenly have a block of maktak," Leavitt says. "It's a whole-year process, from our hunters preparing to go whaling, to them actually being out there with the whale, to the whaling crews working hard to cut the different edible parts. . . . It's coming together with family, it's bringing the community together, serving the people."

The Kims and their kimchi, part of Utqiagvik for more than 40 years, have been welcomed into that community. "Barrow is really magic. People love each other," Louise says. "My hometown is so far away, so these are my people, my village, my family."

JOHN LAST

There Is No Such Thing as Italian Food

FROM *Noema*

ARQUÀ PETRARCA, ITALY—IN the mirror-flat valley of the Po River, the Euganean Hills stick out of the vast landscape, their shallow peaks topped by sloping vineyards and groves of olive trees. Nestled between them is the tiny medieval village of Arquà Petrarca, where a microclimate created by the shaded hills and their abundant water produces perfect conditions for one of Italy's rarest crops.

The giuggiole, or jujube fruit, resembles an olive and tastes, at first, like a woody apple. After withering off the vine, it takes on a sweeter flavor, closer to a honeyed fig. Among the medieval elite, the fruit was so popular that it gave birth to an idiom: "andare in brodo di giuggiole"—"To go in jujube broth"—defined in one of the earliest Italian phrase books as living in a state of bliss. Every fall, the handful of families that still cultivate the fruit in the village gather in medieval garb to celebrate the jujube and feast on the fine liquors, jams, and blissful sweet broth they create from it.

Italy is full of places like Arquà Petrarca. Microclimates and artisanal techniques become the basis for obscure local specialties celebrated in elaborate festivals from Trapani to Trieste. In Mezzago, outside Milan, it's rare pink asparagus, turned red by soil rich in iron and limited sunlight. Sicily has its Avola almonds and peculiar blood-red oranges, which gain their deep color on the volcanic slopes of Mount Etna. Calabria has 'nduja sausage and the Diamante citron, central to the Jewish feast of Sukkot.

All these specialties are encouraged by local cooperatives, protected by local designations, elevated by local chefs and celebrated in local festivals, all lucrative outcomes for their local, often small-scale producers. It's not so much a reflection of capitalismo as campanilismo—a uniquely Italian concept derived from the word for belltower. "It means, if you were born in the shade of the bell-tower, you were from that community," explains Fabio Parasecoli, a professor of food studies at New York University and the author of *Gastronativism,* a new book exploring the intersection of food and politics. "That has translated into food."

In many ways, it's this obsessive focus on the intersection of food and local identity that defines Italy's culinary culture, one that is at once prized the world over and insular in the extreme. After all, campanilismo might be less charitably translated as "provincialism"—a kind of defensive small-mindedness hostile to outside influence and change.

Italy's nativist politicians seek to exploit deep associations between food and identity to present a traditional vision of the country that's at risk of slipping away. In 2011, a politician from the nativist Lega Nord party named Pietro Pezzutti distributed free bags of corn polenta, a northern delicacy, emblazoned with the phrase "yes to polenta, no to couscous"—a swipe at the region's immigrants from Africa, where couscous originates. "We want to make people understand that polenta is part of our history, and must be safeguarded," Pezzutti explained.

All across Italy, as Parasecoli tells me, food is used to identify who is Italian and who is not. But dig a little deeper into the history of Italian cuisine and you will discover that many of today's iconic delicacies have their origins elsewhere. The corn used for polenta, unfortunately for Pezzutti, is not Italian. Neither is the jujube. In fact, none of the foods mentioned above are. All of them are immigrants, in their own way—lifted from distant shores and brought to this tiny peninsula to be transformed into a cornerstone of an ever-changing Italian cuisine.

Today, jujubes are better known as Chinese dates. It was likely in Asia that the plant was first cultivated, and where most are still grown. By the time of the Roman Emperor Augustus, at the turn of the first millennium, the tree had spread to parts of the eastern Mediterranean where, according to local tradition, it furnished the branches for the thorny crown of Jesus Christ. Around the same time, Pliny the Elder tells us, a Roman counselor imported it to Italy.

The Romans were really the first Italian culinary borrowers. In addition to the jujube, they brought home cherries, apricots, and peaches from the corners of their vast empire, Parasecoli tells me. But in the broad sweep of Italian history, it was Arabs, not Romans, who have left the more lasting mark on Italian cuisine.

During some 200 years of rule in Sicily and southern Italy, and the centuries of horticultural experimentation and trade that followed, Arabs greatly expanded the range of ingredients and flavors in the Italian diet. A dizzying array of modern staples can be credited to their influence, including almonds, spinach, artichokes, chickpeas, pistachios, rice, and eggplants.

Arabs also brought with them durum wheat—since 1967, the only legal grain for the production of pasta in Italy. They introduced sugar cane and citrus fruit, laying the groundwork for dozens of local delicacies in the Italian south and inspiring the region's iconic sweet-and-sour agrodolce flavors. Food writers Alberto Capatti and Massimo Montanari argue that Arabs' effect on the Italian palate was as profound as it was in science or medicine—reintroducing lost recipes from antiquity, elevated by novel ingredients and techniques refined in the intervening centuries. In science, this kind of exchange sparked the Renaissance; in food, they argue, one of the world's great cuisines.

Today, in Italy's north, where African influences give way to more continental fare, Italian cuisine leans heavier on crops taken from Indigenous peoples in the Americas: tomatoes, beans, pumpkins, zucchini, peppers, and corn, which is used to make polenta. Cultural exchange moved in the other direction as well. As millions of Italians left for the Americas in the 19th and 20th centuries, Italy's culinary traditions were remixed and revolutionized again. Italian Americans pioneered a cuisine that would become almost unrecognizable to the old country: spaghetti and meatballs, chicken Marsala, fettuccine Alfredo, deep-dish pizza.

Though traditional-minded Italians still scoff at many of these creations, Italian-American culture nevertheless made its way back to influence the old country, as John Mariani writes. Americans' post-war love affair with Italy gave us more than the americano—it kicked the country's cocktail culture into overdrive and poured American products into Italy that still influence cuisine today.

Virtually all Italian recipes for authentic Neapolitan pizza will ask for "Manitoba flour," a nod to a variety of strong flour milled from hearty North American wheat first imported as part of the Marshall Plan. Even Mezzago's pink asparagus may have come from the U.S.—according to local legend, it was first planted by a returning émigré.

This kind of borrowing never stopped. In 1971, an agronomist named Ottavio Cacioppo read about a "mouse plant" from New Zealand and set out to grow it on a drained swamp near Rome. Today, Italy is behind only China and New Zealand for kiwi production. The Latina region where Cacioppo started out was deemed the "Land of the Kiwi" in 2004, and with almost 30,000 acres now in production, the fruit has been graced with protected status as a regional delicacy.

In 2012, though, something began to change for Italy's kiwi farmers. Thousands of acres of plants began to wither and die inexplicably. Ten years later, the mystery disease is still ravaging the country. No one knows why.

The morià, or kiwi death, is not the only disease to threaten beloved Italian delicacies in recent years. This summer, an outbreak of highly infectious African swine fever was found in the country's ample wild boar population, threatening the rural pig farms that produce staples like prosciutto and Parma ham. The threat was great enough to drive Italy's environmental agency to erect a chain-link wall around parts of Rome.

But it's not only disease that is troubling Italy's farmers. "This year we've seen major changes in the climate, with a very dry spring and summer," Cacioppo tells me. "Blooms, vegetative regrowth, fruit development—all had delays and changes. The fruits have not developed as they should have, and we have lost many benefits for the soil."

This past summer, in some parts of Sicily, half of the iconic citrus crop was claimed by the càscola—a term for the sudden and devastating loss of fruit caused by flash floods, hail storms, and crippling drought. Italy's national research council says 70% of the island is at risk of desertification—and it's not alone.

In northern Italy, the drought of 2021 dried up risotto paddies, forced early harvests of tomatoes, and reduced olive oil production by as much as 30%. Coldiretti, the country's largest farmers' union, estimated almost a third of national agricultural production was threatened by climate change.

The problems are bigger than one bad summer. The last seven years have seen a perpetual heatwave and a drought that scientists estimate is the worst in more than 2,000 years. As mountain snows fail to gather and melt and aquifers fail to refill, the landscape of Italy—and its food culture—is changing forever.

Italy is facing other changes, too. Despite a youth-led back-to-the-land movement, its countryside is emptying. The population is declining in about 90% of rural municipalities. Italy has set new record lows for its birth rate every year for the last decade. It's estimated to lose about a fifth of its population by 2070. "A turn-around in the number of births in the years to come appears un-likely," the country's statistics provider reported in an analysis.

In North America, we might expect to make up that difference with increased immigration. But not Italy, a country notoriously hostile to migrants. The number of foreigners allowed to stay has been kept below a symbolic threshold of six million by increasingly unwelcoming immigration policies. An average of just 280,000 mi-grants are welcomed each year—while nearly half as many people leave the country annually.

This is all the more ironic because of the lengthy and major role migrants have played in delivering Italy's now-disappearing iconic foods to the table. In her study of Italy's "slow food" movement, anthropologist Carole Counihan highlights how, by emphasizing ancient tradition and local family lines, Italy's local food culture often disguises the way immigrants have become crucial links in the production of these delicacies—"From the Pakistani and Moroccan butchers preparing prosciutto in Parma, to Sikhs raising and milk-ing cattle in the Val Padana, to Romanians and Albanians herding sheep in the Abruzzo and Sardinia," she writes.

Taken together, Italy's demographic and climate changes herald a profound transition in Italian cuisine. The real question is, will Italians stay bound to invented traditions, or will they embrace their mercurial past?

At his century-old coffee roastery in Sicily, Andrea Morettino can observe firsthand how climate change is ravaging his native land. "We've witnessed the alteration of the traditional seasons, with double and triple blooms," he says. "Nature has given us an incredible signal, and this signal deserves to be listened to and valued."

For the last 30 years, Morettino and his family have been engaged in what he calls a "huge, ambitious, experimental project" to adapt to these changes in their environment. Using heirloom seeds from the botanical gardens in Palermo, his family raised a small crop of coffee plants—the first-ever commercially grown on Italian soil.

Coffee occupies a special place in Italian culture. There's a café on virtually every corner. But it has long been one of the country's biggest food imports—even its diverse climate could not produce a region suited to coffee growing. That is, until elevated temperatures made it possible. Morettino got more than 60 pounds of viable beans last year. This year, he expects more than 100. "Climate change has a fundamental role in these achievements," he tells me.

These are not quantities that will disrupt the coffee import business. But the small scale of Morettino's production is already part of its marketing appeal. Sicilian coffee, Morettino says, like Sicilian wine or oil, is marked by the terroir: "notes of zibibbo wine, carab and jasmine." That makes it a rare and artisanal product. And like many Italian delicacies, Morettino's coffee is primarily intended for local consumption—part of "a short-chain vision, with lower emissions, with fewer logistics and with lower energy costs."

Like Cacioppo and other agricultural visionaries before him, Morettino sees the potential in Sicilian coffee to become a regional delicacy, one that supports dozens of small farmers and maybe, someday, a modest export market. He recognizes that traditional crops could vanish in a generation. "But historically," he says, "you have some fruits or some vegetables that came from other countries that could adapt to a new land, and that became, in time, a symbol of that land. Like citrus, maybe the coffee that came from tropical lands could be a new symbol of a positive future."

Morettino is not the only person thinking this way. Throughout Sicily, farmers are taking advantage of higher temperatures to grow tropical fruit that was not previously viable, like mangos, papaya, avocados, lychee, and miniature bananito bananas. For the moment, it's not clear what role these tropical crops will play in the future of Italian cuisine. Made-in-Italy coffee is one thing. But what about the preparations and recipes that accompany other tropical plants? Will Italians embrace African flavors the way they once embraced Arab ones?

Some shifts may be inevitable. Even in spite of its attitude to immigration, the number of foreigners in Italy increased 400% between 2004 and 2012, including many from West Africa, Bangladesh, and India. They don't only labor on farms to produce food, Parasecoli says—they often prepare it for Italians too, as care workers or home chefs. Maybe, he wonders, variations on traditional dishes will gradually become accepted.

Italian food could open to a wave of culinary transformation, if Italians are receptive to it. In theory, the Italian food philosopher Alex Ravelli Sorini explains, Italian cuisine is "not like a castle . . . but like a field." Despite strongly held traditions, in other words, the only constants in its culinary culture are seasonality and simplicity—a base of three or four fresh local ingredients combined in a manner straightforward enough for a home cook. "It's not important if it changes in aspects," he says. "The 'tradition' is an idea, an invention of the person. . . . 'Tradition' doesn't exist!"

And yet, Italians can be surprisingly dogmatic about simple combinations. Despite a lengthy history of adopting foreign ingredients as their own, as the Italian gastronomer Simone Cinotto writes: "The Italian culinary model seems to resist almost completely the influence of immigrant cuisines."

As Immaculate Ruému, a Nigerian-born, London-trained chef who develops fusion recipes in Milan, puts it, there is "a big barrier that's very difficult to breach" when it comes to introducing Italians to African foods and flavors, even those that can already be produced from local products. "I have to take away the fact that it's Nigerian," she says. She tends to explain the Nigerian heritage of dishes on a tasting menu after customers have eaten, for example. But if they see that story on a menu, she says, most will say, "We just want a classic ravioli."

Instead, she focuses on where the ingredients come from, emphasizing familiar regional delicacies like Piedmontese Fassona beef. Perhaps someday, she could make ogbono soup with Sicilian mango seeds and Calabrian okra, and maybe then it would be easier to sell to Italians.

But there is a deeper philosophical disconnect that makes many other cuisines unfamiliar to the Italian palate. Ruému says Italians tend to look on spices with suspicion, as if using them was a sign that ingredients are less fresh, which closes off a lot of immigrant cuisines.

And then there's the attitude. There's an entire genre of internet comedy about Italians getting angry at improvisations on their food. Incorporating new ingredients and ideas today, Ruému says, will necessitate a new appreciation for the people who brought them to Italy in the first place, and a collaborative spirit that seems hard to achieve in an age of tense politics. "The people you are trying to copy from know better now," she tells me. "Nigerians are not going to let you come and copy-and-paste. We will hold you accountable."

In a decade or two, you may be able to go to a Calabrian avocado festival, or find more than one place serving jollof risotto with ossobuco and plantain (one of Ruému's recipes). "There will be changes," Parasecoli says. "That is inevitable. But I do think there will be an effort to maintain a familiar way of life, for a sense of emotional security, if not anything else. If you see everything changing around you, it's the end of the world—not only the drought, not only the swine fever, but I cannot find my tomatoes. Then everything is really going to hell in a handbasket."

"You Don't Look Anorexic"

FROM *The New York Times Magazine*

SHARON MAXWELL SPENT much of her life trying to make herself small. Her family put her on her first diet when she was 10. Early on Saturday mornings, she and her mother would drive through the empty suburban streets of Hammond, Indiana, to attend Weight Watchers meetings. Maxwell did her best at that age to track her meals and log her points, but the scale wasn't going down fast enough. So she decided to barely eat anything on Fridays and take laxatives that she found in the medicine cabinet.

Food had long been a fraught subject in the Maxwell household. Her parents were also bigger-bodied and dieted frequently. They belonged to a fundamentalist Baptist megachurch where gluttony was seen as a sin. To eat at home was to navigate a labyrinth of rules and restrictions. Maxwell watched one time as her mother lost 74 pounds in six months by consuming little more than carrot juice (her skin temporarily turned orange). Sometimes her father, seized with a new diet idea, abruptly ransacked shelves in the kitchen, sweeping newly forbidden foods into the trash. Maxwell was constantly worried about eating too much. She started to eat alone and in secret. She took to chewing morsels and spitting them out. She hid food behind books, in her pockets, under mattresses and between clothes folded neatly in drawers.

Through Maxwell's teenage years and early 20s, eating became even more stressful. Her thoughts constantly orbited around food: what she was eating or not eating, the calories she was burning or not burning, the size of her body and, especially, what people thought of it. Her appearance was often a topic of public interest.

When she went grocery shopping for her family, other customers commented on the items in her cart. "Honey, are you sure you want to eat that?" one person said. Other shoppers offered unsolicited advice about diets. Strangers congratulated her when her cart was filled with vegetables.

As she grew older, people at the gym clapped and cheered for her while she worked out. "People would say: 'Go! You can lose the weight!'" she says. While eating in public, other diners offered feedback—and still do to this day—on her choices, a few even asking if she wanted to join their gym. Some would call her names: Pig, Fatty. Sometimes people told her she was brave for wearing shorts, while others said she should cover up. She was always aware, whether she wanted to be or not, of how others viewed her body.

Maxwell tried just about every diet she could find: juice cleanses, Atkins, SlimFast, South Beach, Mediterranean, Whole30, and Ezekiel, a regimen based on biblical references. She tried being vegetarian and vegan and paleo. She tried consuming less than 500 calories a day and taking HCG, a fertility hormone rumored to suppress appetite but flagged by the F.D.A. as risky and unproven for weight loss. During periods of religious fasting at her church, she would take the practice to an extreme, consuming nothing but water for days (and on one occasion, two weeks). "I passed out a few times, but I did it," she says. Sometimes she exercised more than three hours a day in high-intensity interval-training sessions and kickboxing classes. Eventually, she started vomiting up her food.

Every day, Maxwell stepped on the scale and internalized the number as a reflection of her self-worth. Often, the number on the scale went down. But if she let up on her rigid food rules even briefly, the number shot back up like a coiled spring. "I just cycled through that," she says, "but it became harder and harder each time to get the weight off."

During the many years of dieting and deprivation, Maxwell experienced mysterious health problems. For a decade, starting when she was 16, she almost never had her period. She was always cold. She often had dizzy spells and occasionally passed out in class. When she was in college, she fainted three times in one day and was taken to the emergency room. For an appointment with an endocrinologist one year, Maxwell took a purse full of small plastic bags. Each one contained a day's worth of hair, clumps that accumulated in her brush or had fallen in the shower drain. Her head was pocked with bald spots. The doctor was pleased with her weight loss and, to her memory, didn't seem too concerned about her other symptoms. "Anything that made the scale go down," Maxwell says, "I was given a pat on the back."

Four years ago, at the age of 25, Maxwell walked into her primary-care doctor's office near Scottsdale, Arizona, where she lived and worked as a middle school teacher. She was there for an annual physical, and she was prepared to be told to lose weight, as she had almost always been instructed. But this time, the doctor, an osteopath, started asking unusual questions. Maxwell's blood work showed abnormally low iron and electrolyte levels. The doctor asked Maxwell what she was eating and what she was doing in relationship to food. Was she starving herself? Was she vomiting on purpose? Maxwell was surprised by this line of questioning. "These are things I had hidden my whole life from my family, my friends, doctors," she says.

The osteopath told her she thought Maxwell had an eating disorder and suggested arranging treatment right away. Maxwell would later be diagnosed with atypical anorexia nervosa, an increasingly common yet little known eating disorder that shares all the same symptoms as anorexia nervosa, except for extreme thinness. Just as many people, and possibly many more, suffer from atypical anorexia.

At the physical, Maxwell stared at her doctor in disbelief. She always thought that eating disorders were for skinny people. "I laughed," she says. "I don't use language like this any longer, but I told her she was crazy. I told her, 'No, I have a self-control problem.'"

For centuries, the eating disorder that would become known as anorexia nervosa mystified the medical community, which struggled to understand, or even define, an illness that caused people to deliberately deprive themselves of food. As cases rose over the course of the 19th and 20th centuries, anorexia was considered a purely psychological disorder akin to hysteria. Sir William Withey Gull, an English physician who coined the term "anorexia nervosa" in the late 1800s, called it a perversion of the ego. In 1919, after an autopsy revealed an atrophied pituitary gland, anorexia was thought to be an endocrinological disease. That theory was later debunked, and in the mid-20th century, psychoanalytic explanations arose, pointing to sexual and developmental dysfunction and, later, unhealthy family dynamics. More recently, the medical field has come to believe that anorexia can be the product of a constellation of psychological, social, genetic, neurological, and biological factors.

Since anorexia nervosa became the first eating-related disorder listed in the Diagnostic and Statistical Manual of Mental Disorders in 1952, its criteria have shifted as well. Initially, anorexia had no weight criteria and was classified as a psychophysiological disorder. In a 1972 paper, a team led by the prominent psychiatrist John Feighner suggested using a weight loss of at least 25 percent as a standard for research purposes, and in 1980, the D.S.M. introduced that figure in its definition (along with a criterion that patients weigh well below "normal" for their age and height, although normal was not defined). Doctors who relied on that number soon found that patients who had lost at least 25 percent of their body weight were already severely sick, so in 1987, the diagnosis was revised to include those who weighed less than 85 percent of their "normal" body weight (what qualified as normal was left to physicians to decide). In the 2013 D.S.M., the criteria shifted again, characterizing those who suffer from anorexia as having a "significantly low weight," a description that would also appear in the 2022 edition.

In that 2013 edition, a new diagnosis appeared—atypical anorexia nervosa—after health care providers noticed more patients showing up for treatment with all the symptoms of anorexia nervosa except one: a significantly low weight. Those with atypical anorexia, doctors observed, suffer the same mental and physical symptoms as people with anorexia nervosa, even life-threatening heart issues and electrolyte imbalances. They restrict calories intensively; obsess about food, eating, and body image; and view their weight as inextricably linked to their value. They often skip meals, eat in secret, adhere to intricate rules about what foods they allow themselves to consume, and create unusual habits like chewing and spitting out food. Others exercise to the point of exhaustion, abuse laxatives or purge their meals. But unlike those diagnosed with anorexia, people with atypical anorexia can lose significant amounts of weight but still have a medium or large body size. Others, because of their body's metabolism, hardly lose any weight at all. To the outside world, they appear "overweight."

Starting in the mid-2000s, the number of people seeking treatment for the disorder rose sharply. Whether more people are developing atypical anorexia or seeking treatment—or more doctors are recognizing it—is unknown, but this group now comprises up to half of all patients hospitalized in eating-disorder programs. Studies suggest that the same number of people, even as many as three times as many, will develop atypical anorexia as traditional anorexia in their lifetimes. One high estimate suggests that as much as 4.9 percent of the female population will have the disorder. For boys, the number is lower—one estimate was 1.2 percent. For men, it is likely even lower, though little research exists. For nonbinary people, the number jumps to as high as 7.5 percent.

Across the board, the pandemic exacerbated eating disorders, including typical and atypical anorexia, through increased isolation, heightened anxiety, and disrupted routines. Hospitals and outpatient clinics in the United States and abroad reported the number of consultations and admissions doubling and tripling during Covid lockdowns, and many providers are still overbooked. "Almost all of my colleagues, we're at capacity," says Shira Rosenbluth, an eating-disorder therapist who specializes in size- and gender-diverse clients. They are seeing clients who practice more extreme food restriction and experience more intense distress around body image and eating habits. "The demand has increased, the level of severity has increased," Rosenbluth says. "We've never seen waiting lists like this for treatment centers."

Despite its prevalance, atypical anorexia is still considered widely underdiagnosed and under-researched, and many primary-care doctors have never heard of it. "Some people being at a standard body weight or overweight can be perplexing to the untrained eye," says Karlee McGlone, senior manager of admissions and outreach for U.C. San Diego Health Eating Disorders Center. "It is still a surprise for nonspecialized clinicians."

Patients, too, are in the dark about atypical anorexia. "Most people in higher-weight bodies are shocked to hear that they have anorexia," says Rachel Millner, a psychologist based in Pennsylvania who specializes in eating disorders among people with larger bodies. "Nobody ever told them that you can be in a higher-weight body and have anorexia, and they're convinced that their problem is their weight."

In 2020, Erin Harrop, an assistant professor of social work at the University of Denver, completed a survey of 39 people with atypical anorexia, most of whom were obese, and found that participants endured the disorder for an average of 11.6 years before seeking help. They lost an average of 64 pounds, and a quarter of the group had yet to receive treatment. (By comparison, the treatment delays for anorexia are, on average, 2.5 years; for bulimia, 4.4 years; and for binge-eating disorder, 5.6 years, according to a 2021 review.)

To make it easier for people with atypical anorexia to be screened, treated, and insured, there's a growing movement in the field to collapse the categories of anorexia and atypical anorexia into one—to no longer see them as separate illnesses, to decouple anorexia from its virtually synonymous association with thinness. "For years, we have thought about anorexia nervosa in one way," says Carolyn Costin, an eating-disorder therapist who founded an eating-disorder treatment center and is a co-author of *8 Keys to Recovery from an Eating Disorder*. "But the way people think about it and how they want to define it is changing. It would be a paradigm shift within the field."

Many, however, are fiercely resistant to letting go of the metric of weight. It would require altering the organizing principle by which the public and the greater medical field conceive of the condition. It would also require recognizing that anyone, in any body, can starve themselves into poor health—and you'd never know it by looking at them.

It took Maxwell a long time to process that she had an eating disorder. She had been so steeped in the gospel of dieting that it was hard to accept that restricting her food was not unequivocally healthy. But as her doctor instructed, she began making visits to the hospital for intravenous fluids and started taking iron supplements. At night, she began attending outpatient sessions at Liberation Center, a now-shuttered facility in Phoenix, where she ate dinner with other clients and attended group therapy. The staff at Liberation told her she needed more intensive treatment and recommended attending a residential program.

In the summer of 2018, after teaching through the rest of the school year, Maxwell agreed to go to a center in Monterey, California, that was covered by her insurance. A day after she arrived, however, her insurance rescinded approval: Because of her weight, the company didn't believe she was sick enough to meet the criteria for residential care for eating disorders. She was at once ashamed and incensed. Her aunt drove five hours to pick her up, and she spent much of the next 10 days on the phone with the insurance company.

Her insurance eventually authorized her to go to another facility, the Center for Discovery Rancho Palos Verdes, which sits on the Southern California coast. Maxwell's three-month stay would consist of group meals, outings to restaurants to practice dining in public settings, yoga, and therapy. "I went with the expectation that as soon as I walked in the door, they would be the people who would help me finally become thin once and for all," she says. Instead, on her first day, a dietitian at the center explained that she would need to eat three balanced meals and three snacks a day to recover. Her treatment plan also required that she abstain from almost all forms of exercise so her system could recalibrate. Maxwell panicked. She had never consistently eaten that much in her entire adult life, and she still felt that her body was a problem to be fixed.

Maxwell already harbored a deep mistrust of the mental-health profession. When she was growing up, she remembers a pastor at her church preaching that psychiatry was the work of the devil. The message seemed to be that anxiety was sinful, a sign of faithlessness. Maxwell had left her church two years earlier, but its lessons were still lodged deeply in her mind. She couldn't abandon her long-held belief, one that her doctors reinforced for much of her life, that thinness was the primary measure of health.

Maxwell forced herself to go along with each step of the treatment program. She tried to eat three meals and three snacks a day, even though it caused her excruciating fear. For years, her thinking had revolved tightly around food and exercise; and during twice-weekly individual therapy sessions and daily group therapy, she tried to learn how to redirect these thoughts. She started to talk about the self-judgment, shame, and childhood trauma that led to rigid behaviors and an overreliance on control, both central features of restrictive eating disorders.

About five or six weeks into treatment, it dawned on her just how much damage she had done to herself. Her esophagus burned from years of purging. She experienced heart palpitations and was often dizzy from orthostatic hypotension (a type of low blood pressure that leads to dizziness and fainting), and her hair and nails were thin and brittle from malnutrition. "I started to realize, holy shit, this is real," she says. "I started to see what it had done to my body, the magnitude of it."

Over the ensuing weeks, Maxwell began eating enough food that the staff allowed her to go on walks and swim, not to burn calories but as a part of learning how to live a balanced life. Her physical symptoms started to ease. Her vital signs and blood work improved. She felt less dizzy, her heartbeat more regular. She got her period back for the first time in a decade. And perhaps most surprising, she was not gaining weight despite eating more food.

To help her overcome her self-judgment, a nurse suggested that she look in the mirror and express what she liked about her body. At first, Maxwell couldn't think of what to say. She could hardly make eye contact with her own reflection. But eventually she thought of something. "I'm grateful for my curly hair," she said, looking at the nurse in the mirror.

When a human body is starved for long enough, it undergoes a complex series of biological, metabolic, and hormonal changes to ensure its own survival. Every system moves to conserve energy, and the body begins to mine muscle and fat for glucose to keep the heart running and the brain functioning. The metabolism slows, which is why some people can eat very little and hardly lose any weight. Digestion simmers down, sometimes causing gastro-intestinal trouble, and body temperature plummets while blood flow decreases. Many people who chronically undereat shiver with cold, their hands and feet feeling especially icy. If malnutrition worsens, their hair becomes fragile and falls out and muscle mass dwindles, including within the heart.

People with severe anorexia of any kind can have orthostatic hypotension, heart rates lower than 60 beats per minute and electrolyte imbalances that may cause arrhythmias or even lead to cardiac arrest. Eventually a malnourished body can shut down the production of sex hormones. From what little research on atypical anorexia exists, the medical complications appear to be the same as anorexia and occur in similar rates across body sizes, with the exceptions of bone density loss and low blood sugar, which are worse in those who are emaciated. Recent research has found that body size is a less relevant indicator of the severity of both eating disorders than other factors, including the percentage of body mass lost, the speed of that loss, and the duration of the malnourished state.

Among scientists, there is consensus that atypical anorexia and anorexia share the same medical and nutritional issues, but one of the big remaining questions is whether the psychopathology is the same (some clinicians believe that it is, but minimal research exists to confirm this). In the slim populations they have studied, psychologists have observed a grim momentum to the illness: Sufferers lose just a few pounds and then, all of the sudden, they compulsively want to lose more, as if a mental switch flips. Genetic predispositions may explain why some people lose weight and their minds tip into disordered eating while others do not. Immediate female family members of a patient with anorexia nervosa are 11 times as likely to develop it as females in the general population, according to one study.

In the short term, resisting hunger pangs can make people feel powerful and even euphoric. But soon the effects of starvation on the brain set in: mental fog, difficulty concentrating, memory issues. People become secretive, irritable and inflexible in their thinking. The gray matter of the brain shrinks, and it appears that the neural pathways related to rewards can be reversed. (It's not clear if that's a pre-existing trait or an effect of the illness.) Food that typically results in a dopamine hit now inspires dread. The crippling fear of weight gain begins to outcompete the biological urge to eat, spiraling downward into more weight loss and distorted thinking.

In a famed 1944 study known as the Starvation Experiment, Prof. Ancel Keys of the University of Minnesota and his team observed the impact of food deprivation on people's relationship to eating. They persuaded 36 young, healthy men to undergo six months of semi-starvation and five months of resumed feeding to determine the best means for treating people who suffered famine and forced starvation in World War II. The men lost 25 percent of their body weight. And over the course of the study, these otherwise mentally fit young participants developed many of the symptoms of anorexia, bulimia, and binge-eating disorder, including obsession with eating, cutting food into small pieces, bingeing and purging, excruciatingly slow eating and, even five months after they regained weight, body-image issues. More recent research suggests that losing just 5 percent of one's body weight can be associated with a clinically significant eating disorder.

Because of the complex interplay between the physical and mental symptoms of starvation, the first steps to recovery for people with malnutrition are to eat more and to gain weight, a process called refeeding or renourishment, before working on the behavioral and cognitive aspects of the disease. But for people who are acutely ill, eating too much too fast increases the risk of potentially fatal fluid and electrolyte imbalances that can develop in malnourished bodies. Specific protocols govern how people with anorexia are refed, and research is still emerging on how to renourish people with atypical anorexia.

A 2019 study led by Andrea K. Garber, a professor of pediatrics and chief nutritionist for the Eating Disorder Program at U.C. San Francisco, found that when atypical anorexia patients were given the same high-calorie foods in the same portions as anorexia patients, they did not recover as well. "It might sound like a no-brainer," Garber says. "They have a larger body size, and so we believe they need more nutrition to recover."

But clinicians, many of whom have been trained to focus on weight as a predominant health measure, have to navigate how best to advise patients who face both the perils of a potentially fatal restrictive eating disorder and the health risks associated with larger body sizes. In one case study, for example, a 15-year-old girl with atypical anorexia had stopped having her period and was hospitalized for severe malnutrition and bradycardia, a dangerously slow heart rate. Refeeding helped her recover from her eating disorder, but then she lost her period again because of polycystic ovarian syndrome, a condition that occurs in people of all sizes but is more common and often more severe in people who have higher percentages of body fat.

Some psychologists report that atypical anorexia is harder to treat than anorexia nervosa because the fear of weight gain is even greater in people who have been bullied and shamed for their size. The biggest difference in the two conditions, some psychologists believe, may be how they are perceived by the outside world, biases that persist even in places where patients go to seek help.

After she left the Center for Discovery Rancho Palos Verdes and moved to South Carolina, Maxwell started a partial hospitalization program at the Eating Recovery Center in Greenville. She immediately began noticing how her size was affecting the quality of her treatment. When she arrived, a staff member put her in a room and told her to wait, while the people with "normal" eating disorders gathered next door. Her words felt like a gut punch. At lunch, she was told to sit by herself at the back of the dining room, while the other clients sat together with their backs to her. "I was like, I can't sit with them?" she says. The center had mistaken her diagnosis for binge-eating disorder and had a policy of separating those clients from the others.

Sometimes staff members singled her out and had her eat less than small-bodied patients. At a group-therapy session in which she was the only large person in the room, another patient shared that she would rather die than be fat. "Her literally expressing that while I'm in that room—that to be me, to live in this body that I have to recover in, would be worse than anything—it's just ostracizing," Maxwell says. (The Eating Recovery Center does not comment on individual patient experiences, but since 2021, it says, it has made efforts to counteract weight stigma in its treatment centers.)

Erin Harrop, the social-work professor, who uses they/them pronouns, has experienced both ends of the treatment spectrum for eating disorders. They attended treatment for anorexia in their early 20s with a small body; then, several years later, they returned for treatment for atypical anorexia. Harrop was shocked by the differences. Even though they had been diagnosed with atypical anorexia, had lost nearly 20 percent of their body weight and were experiencing orthostatic blood pressure, the therapist at the treatment center did not believe their diagnosis and even encouraged them to compare themselves to "sicker" residents—those with smaller bodies. Comments about their body from doctors, dietitians and other professionals exacerbated their disordered thinking. They were bullied by peers for their weight, and the kitchen staff limited their food intake: When their peers ate bagels, they received a bite-size one.

In their 2020 survey of people with atypical anorexia, Harrop discovered that every participant had also been overlooked, misdiagnosed, or excluded. Almost everyone had approached medical providers with symptoms of malnutrition, like hair loss, dropped periods, fainting, vomiting blood, or dry or bleeding skin. But it took years, and sometimes decades, for anyone to screen them for an eating disorder. As a teenager, one participant, Eli, believed she had an eating issue and approached her doctor about it. The physician disagreed, instead telling her that she "could actually probably lose a little bit of weight," she said. It took eight more years before Eli began treatment for atypical anorexia. Another participant, Lexi, remembered a physician telling her: "You don't look anorexic. You don't look underweight."

Tori, also a participant, was diagnosed by her therapist but was then denied treatment referrals by her physician, who said she was too overweight. Layla, who consumed nothing but bone broth and lost 22 percent of their body weight, was diagnosed with "compulsive eating." Two participants had been hospitalized for being suicidal and for their eating-disorder symptoms but were barred from joining an eating-disorder support group because, they were told, they were too large. One participant, while seeking treatment at a center for eating disorders, was given a diet book.

Shira Rosenbluth, the eating-disorder therapist, has struggled with atypical anorexia and says treatment actually made her sicker. At one center, a nurse insisted that she had a food addiction and continually commented on her meals, which were dictated by the dietitian. The nurse recommended Overeaters Anonymous and the controversial GreySheet diet, a low-carb, no-sugar, no-alcohol regimen for people who compulsively overeat, even though Rosenbluth had lost significant weight. At various points, she experienced orthostatic blood pressure and abnormally low phosphorus, which can cause bone pain, irregular breathing, numbness, or heart failure. Blood work showed that her pancreas wasn't functioning properly. Still, she was given less food than smaller-bodied patients. At another center, when patients had ice cream cones, she got a kid-size one.

For two years, she went from treatment center to treatment center, hoping that each one would be better than the last. Finally, she gave up altogether and stayed with a friend, a psychologist in the field, who oversaw her meals and helped her become more stable. "For the first time," she says, "I was getting care without a stigma attached."

In recognition of the inconsistent care that people with atypical anorexia sometimes receive, a small vanguard of professionals in the field are experimenting with ways to improve treatment for people with larger bodies. Erin Harrop runs weight-stigma training sessions for treatment centers, hospitals, and social-work graduate students. Lisa Brownstone, an assistant professor at the University of Denver, is piloting psychotherapy groups for eating-disorder patients who have been traumatized by weight stigma. Centers like Opal: Food and Body Wisdom in Seattle have hired body-diverse staff members, created physical spaces that accommodate a range of bodies, and trained therapists on size inclusivity. But there's only so much they can do before butting up against systemic challenges, and the biggest one is discriminatory insurance coverage.

Some atypical anorexia patients are authorized for treatment for only two or three weeks before they are cut off—an almost impossibly short period of time to recover. Certain insurance companies outright deny coverage for people with larger bodies. Lexi Giblin, Opal's executive director, has seen some patients with atypical anorexia not receive authorization for treatment even though they have the same symptoms as someone with a smaller body. "The invalidation of the insurance company can certainly contribute to the symptoms themselves," Giblin says. "They can become part of the eating disorder. We've had folks who are denied authorization then come back later, and their eating disorder has escalated since the last time we saw them. That's pretty common."

The issue stems not only from a lack of knowledge about a relatively new diagnosis; it's also a product of how the diagnosis is named and coded. Because it is labeled "atypical" and filed under the murky "other specified feeding or eating disorder" category, it is often seen as less dangerous. "It's an absurd diagnosis," says Jennifer L. Gaudiani, an internist who specializes in eating disorders in Denver and the author of *Sick Enough: A Guide to the Medical Complications of Eating Disorders.* "There's nothing atypical about it. If there's anything atypical, it's the people who get underweight."

To make it easier for people to secure care, some therapists, social workers, and researchers have been advocating combining atypical anorexia and anorexia by removing the requirement to have a "significantly low weight" from the standard anorexia diagnosis. But the idea of merging the categories has ignited strong feelings within the field, with fierce support by people with larger bodies who have suffered from weight discrimination, and incredulous opposition (largely behind closed doors) among some researchers who have devoted their careers to the illness as it is currently described.

Opponents argue that such a change would be premature; much remains unknown about atypical anorexia, including its brain biology, genetics, and psychopathology, all of which could help inform treatment and the development of drugs. (To date, there are no pharmacological treatments for anorexia.) Distinguishing between the two, they say, is crucial to studying them effectively. "It is not helpful to us if we put the atypical anorexia nervosa folks in exactly the same bucket as the typical anorexia nervosa," says Guido Frank, a psychiatry professor at U.C. San Diego who specializes in the brain biology of eating disorders. "I'm not saying they're any less ill—that's the last thing I want to say. To define and devise the right treatments for each of the subgroups, we're best advised that we also study them in a way separately or along a trajectory."

But proponents of the change say that the weight requirement for anorexia causes those with medium and larger bodies to be excluded from many studies. They also point out that the line between the two diagnoses is not particularly scientific and has harmful effects on patients' ability to secure care. "From my personal patient experience," Harrop says, "at no point was there a magic switch where it was like, oh, now I'm atypical. I notice such a difference in my thoughts than I did when I was 10 pounds lighter. To draw this line in the sand of this is when it crosses over and becomes more important and more insurable and more lethal—that line is not a very good line. It always means there's an out group, and it always means that there's somebody who's not able to get treatment. So thinking about how we draw those lines is really important in terms of health equity."

Harrop argues that the anorexia diagnosis could be structured as a spectrum, with weight as one component but not the predominant one. Physicians could look at a wider set of factors when screening, diagnosing, and treating eating disorders. Eating-disorder diagnoses have overlapping symptoms anyway, Harrop says, and patients often cross over between illnesses. About 36 percent of people with anorexia develop bulimia at some point, and 27 percent of people with bulimia develop anorexia, according to one study.

Diagnoses affect not only how doctors and insurance companies categorize patients but also how people understand their own illnesses. Maxwell always bristles when she thinks about her own diagnosis, her mind snagging on the term "atypical." She sometimes flashes to a moment in junior high school when her teacher showed the class a photo of a fat man with a shirt that read, "I beat anorexia." It was meant to be a joke, and everyone laughed. She even laughed. But after a lifetime of bullying, Maxwell didn't want to be a punchline. Being labeled "atypical" added another layer of awkwardness and marginalization. The diagnosis seems to live in a no man's land of categorization. Many people who suffer from eating disorders say the differentiation further perpetuates a social hierarchy. Just as living in a thin body comes with certain privileges, anorexia itself lives at the top of a kind of disordered-eating class system.

According to Mimi Cole, a therapist who had atypical anorexia and hosts "The Lovely Becoming," a mental-health podcast, "A common belief among people with atypical anorexia—and I shared this too—is: I need to lose more weight so that I have anorexia, so that I can be sicker. I can meet criteria. I can have a real eating disorder."

In late 2018, Maxwell decided to be more open about her eating disorder with friends and family and started posting about it on Instagram. Over the years, she included photographs of her younger self and shared memories of her decades-long journey. Sometimes it felt brazen and edgy, but also good. "I am fat and I have anorexia," she wrote in a 2020 post. "And I don't have to explain my body to you."

These days, Maxwell's inner landscape is very different than it once was. On a sunny Saturday afternoon in May, not far from where she lives in San Diego, she did something that would have brought her waves of anxiety in past years. She went to the beach. Amid the tinny jangle of an ice cream truck, she unfurled her towel and sat down. Before she started her recovery, she would have spent her time at the beach worried about what she was wearing or not wearing, what she had eaten or would eat later and what other people were thinking or not thinking about her body. Fogged by this tangle of thoughts, she would miss the experience. Now she doesn't give those things much thought. On that Saturday, she watched her dog zoom around the sand and laughed with a couple of friends. Her mind was not floating above her body, dissociated.

Maxwell is choosing to recover as fully as she can, but it is not easy. After 19 years of going undiagnosed, she still suffers from some of the physical, mental, and social costs of anorexia. Doctors are monitoring her recovery from long QT syndrome, an electrical issue with the heart that can turn into potentially fatal arrhythmias. (Long QT syndrome is a rare side effect of anorexia.) She also has an annual endoscopy to assess the slow healing of her damaged esophagus from years of vomiting. She has incurred mountains of debt from months of treatment.

She checks in with a doctor and a therapist regularly and texts photos of her meals to her dietitian as proof that she's eating three meals a day, a standard in recovery. She attends an eating-disorder support group, even though she has rarely seen another larger-bodied person there. She has also started to cook for herself. But to be a larger person in this world is to be constantly reminded of how other people view your body.

Often when she posts about recovery and fat positivity on Insta-gram or TikTok, whether it's theatrically smashing her scale with a baseball bat or performing slam poetry in her car, a flurry of trolls rise from the backwaters of the internet to riddle her feed with insults and death threats. "You need a sign that says 'beware of pig,'" one commenter wrote. "Moo moo goes the cow," wrote another who created a handle (@sharon_maxwell_hater) expressly to bully her. "Society pities you because you're eating yourself to an early grave," another wrote.

But Maxwell has also received direct messages from people who have struggled in similar ways—they have never admitted to them-selves, let alone their families or friends, how much they are suf-fering. "I just wanted to say that I am a fat person with an eating disorder who isn't yet in recovery but trying," one wrote. "Every day I have these crazy disordered thoughts and get into a spiral of how I'm not valid enough for recovery . . . your content has been absolutely pivotal for me and I am so happy you exist."

Many people with anorexia describe the illness as a battle be-tween two selves. One is a maniacal superego, hellbent on con-trol at all costs in a misguided attempt to find safety. It imposes perfectionistic rules and restrictions in Sisyphean pursuit of an unreachable ideal. Some feel it is intent on self-destruction. This self, which Maxwell calls the conceptualized self, enforces all the expectations of one's upbringing and the culture at large and sees the world in lifeless tones of black and white, like an old TV.

The second is what Maxwell calls the authentic self. For her, it's the self that spontaneously breaks into impromptu dance moves and wears T-shirts that read, "Don't be a butthole to yourself" and "Therapy is cool." This self has a penchant for gold glitter and animal print and signs up for a rec basketball team on a whim, something she would never have allowed herself to do before. She can eat strawberries or a sandwich or an ice cream cone in public. This self is no longer concerned with being quiet and obedient or apologizing for her existence. And, perhaps most important, she has no interest in making herself small.

KAYLA STEWART

Teach a Man to Fish

FROM *Gravy*

CAPTAIN FREDERICK DOUGLAS McBride IV is probably the only Black commercial fisherman who works along the Texas Gulf Coast. If you know about another one, please tell me. I'd love to meet him, too.

Captain Fred is one of more than half a million Black people in Houston, the nation's fourth-largest city. If you know my hometown, and Captain Fred's, you know about the imprint of Black people on our city. You'll see that imprint in the jazz shows that fill up clubs downtown, in the Creole and Cajun seafood joints that line the city's strip malls, and in the soul food restaurants that bring you close to the feeling of eating in your aunt's kitchen. What you may not know is that Black folks govern our city, from school boards to our mayor. This legacy stretches back through Houston's history—the city simply wouldn't be what it is without generations of Black residents leaving their mark.

Today, Captain Fred is one of a community of Black Houstonians shaping what the city eats. And in the years to come, his vision is to cultivate the next generation of men and women who catch our fish.

Captain Fred remembers learning to fish at age four, alongside his brother, Jesse. Their grandfather would take the boys out to the 61st Street Fishing Pier on Galveston Bay, about an hour's drive from their home. Young Fred's first catch was a piggy perch.

From the beginning, fishing with his grandfather shifted something in Fred's soul. The water felt like a natural home, and as he cast he imagined the world that existed beneath the surface.

As he grew up and spent more time on the Bay, he learned about discipline, about the environment, and about the man he wanted to become. Years would pass before he would dream of calling this love his profession.

According to the U.S. Bureau of Labor Statistics, approximately 35,000 Americans work as commercial fishermen and -women. Of those, we don't know how many are Black. But we do know they are few. In 2017, commercial fishermen harvested almost 10 billion pounds of seafood from U.S. waters, realizing some five billion dollars in profit. Today, the commercial fishing industry is overwhelmingly white. But this was not always a white vocation.

I asked Captain Fred why he believed he was the only Black fisherman in the region. Thoughtfully he paused, rummaged through his mind, and then looked directly at me. He told me, "I believe I'm the only Black one because of the access, and because of the fact that people don't know that this opportunity exists." For him, learning how to fish as a child, and later learning to navigate the complicated (and expensive) roads to boat ownership and business ownership, allowed him to become who he is today. Like all of us, his path was shaped by environments both built and natural, and by the people who moved through those environments with him. But Fred acknowledges that his story is not common for many people who look like him.

Captain Fred's maternal grandfather, Jesse Lundy, worked as a sharecropper in Bailey's Prairie, south of Houston. He told his grandsons harrowing stories about long, hot days, his hands pricked from cotton bolls. Lundy was able to leave the fields and went to college at Houston College for Negroes (now Texas Southern University). He earned both a bachelor's and a master's degree and eventually became a school principal. His career as an educator helped him achieve the financial stability that allowed for activities outside of work. He could afford to fish recreationally, and it became his great love.

Fred's mother, Jessica McBride, didn't fish, but she became an educator like her father, and she shared her family's other great passion—music. Mrs. McBride directed the band at B.C. Elmore Middle School in Houston for twenty-seven years. For the McBride family, music and fishing have long intersected. For at least the last three generations, both have provided joy, a sense of freedom, and at times a source of income.

When Jesse Lundy died, Fred was thirteen years old and his brother was eleven. His last words to his grandsons were "I love you boys," and "Now remember, we're going fishing on Saturday." Lundy didn't make it to that next fishing trip, but the McBride brothers' time on the water would continue.

Jessica McBride could've easily allowed the hobby to drift away, but she saw how integral fishing had become to the boys' lives. Early on weekend mornings, they'd leave their home in Houston to fish along Galveston Bay while their mother would wait in the car, reading or taking a nap.

Both Fred and his brother studied for careers in music education. Jesse, a jazz pianist, teaches in the Black American Music program at Tulane University. He often comes back home to fish. A classically trained musician, Fred played weddings as part of a string quartet during graduate school. The money from those gigs supported his fishing habit. Fred taught music in downtown Houston for eighteen years, primarily at MacGregor Elementary School.

Though Fred has left the school district to fish full-time, I met him one rainy afternoon in the classroom where he used to teach his young students about classical composers, jazz artists, and reading and playing music. He told me how he views fishing, too, through the lens of education. He wants other Black people, especially youth, to know that fishing can be a hobby. Or it can be a career. Black knowledge is at the root of his quest.

While Captain Fred has carved out an unusual niche for himself as a Black Texan commercial fisherman, his journey points to universal truths about the Black experience in the American South. And that story, of course, goes back to the West African coast.

Centuries ago, along Ghana's Gold Coast, fishermen were revered. European voyagers recognized the skills of the Fanti and Mina of the Gold Coast and the Kru of what is now Liberia. Harvard researcher Emmanuel Akyeampong found that European ship captains regularly recruited Mina and Kru fishermen to work canoes and load and offload goods. The ingenuity of Black fishermen reportedly baffled many of the newly arrived Europeans.

Male Akro was one such fisherman. Recalled in Teshi and Labadi accounts, he introduced several new kinds of nets to the Ga people during the nineteenth century, including the *tengiraf,* a bottom net that "stretched along the coast in the sea as the telegraph wires on the land," and could catch an astounding number of fish. Other Africans, particularly the Fanti, introduced Europeans to their particular styles of nets and canoe-like boats.

Many Africans enslaved in the South originated from that coast. While the specifics have mostly been lost to history, we do know that Africans were much more likely than English colonizers to have hunting and fishing experience. During the plantation period, African Americans were virtually the only marine fishermen.

In a case study focused on coastal Georgia, researcher Ben G. Blount found that slave owners encouraged enslaved people to fish to supplement their food supplies. Using dugout canoes and later, wooden boats, enslaved people on the Georgia Sea Islands obtained half of their meat from fishing. Post-enslavement, small-scale fishing provided an economic opportunity for Blacks. Whether hauling in a cast net full of fish or pulling a waterlogged crab trap, this was physically demanding work. But it was a source of income, and of independence.

Into the twentieth century, Black Americans dominated the oyster, shrimp, and blue crab industries in South Carolina and Georgia. They profited from fish and other seafood along the Gulf Coast of Texas and Louisiana. But as national demand for seafood increased, newly arrived European immigrants began to take an interest in the industry. They brought in larger, more expensive boats and equipment, taking advantage of costly new technology. They opened canneries to process their catch on a larger scale. Their practices tended to be less sustainable, often leading to overfishing and environmental degradation. By and large, Black commercial fishermen could no longer afford to compete, often because they lacked access to the bank loans necessary to finance a commercial boat with up-to-date equipment. Some went to work for larger operations, earning wages instead of the profits of ownership. One study found that, as of 1999, only five Black shrimpers on the Georgia coast owned and operated their own boats.

Black fishermen helped shape and define fishing culture in the South, yet their contributions are rarely acknowledged. Today, few have access to the financial capital necessary to continue this legacy. Still, their work is evident in our regional cuisine. Shrimp and grits was born of enslaved Africans augmenting their rations with shrimp they caught themselves. Frogmore Stew, full of heavily seasoned shrimp and crabs, takes its name from the Gullah-Geechee community on St. Helena Island, South Carolina, where it likely originated.

Today, along the coasts of South Carolina and Georgia, many Gullah-Geechee people work to maintain the fishing traditions of their communities. They work in harvesting, cast-net making, and boat-building; and they continue to catch shad, crabs, oysters, shrimp, and more. Queen Quet, a conservationist and Chieftess of the Gullah-Geechee nation, has participated in oyster replanting efforts across the Sea Islands. The community does this work in spite of external challenges like gentrification and climate change.

The connection between Black Americans and the water has been fraught since the beginning of the Transatlantic Slave Trade. A brutal, horrific journey across the Atlantic Ocean that included drownings and suicides marked a new relationship to the water.

Water became racialized in the United States. In the Jim Crow South, Black Americans were blocked from public beaches and pools. Later, the desegregation of public swimming spaces was sometimes marked by violence. Other times, venues were closed altogether.

In 1959, Gilbert R. Mason Sr. began leading a series of "wade-ins" on the beach in Biloxi, Mississippi, facing down assault and arrest. During one wade-in in 1960, a white mob attacked 125 Black men, women, and children as police officers watched.

In 1964, civil rights activists orchestrated by Martin Luther King Jr. conducted a swim-in at the Monson Motor Lodge in St. Augustine, Florida. Black protestors, disgusted with ongoing segregation, jumped into the hotel's whites-only pool. The motel's owner, James Brock, retaliated by pouring acid in the water.

Research shows that the relationship between Black Americans and the water is still fraught. In 2010, a USA Swimming survey found that 70 percent of Black children had low or no swimming ability. Yet to work on the water, it's imperative to know how to swim.

Today, groups like Brown Folks Fishing, Ebony Anglers, and the International Federation of Black Bass Anglers work as a corrective to some of the more traumatic aspects of Black history with the water. They use recreational fishing as a tool to repair the fraught relationship between Black Americans and the water.

For Captain Fred, recreational fishing tournaments were the bridge between fishing as a hobby and fishing as a business. In the mid-2000s, he placed fourth in the Gulf Coast Trout Masters and competed successfully in redfish tournaments, too. But his wife was concerned. He was spending a lot of money to enter competitions, but he wasn't bringing anything in. That's when he got the idea for Captain Fred's Seafood. Hoping to leave a legacy for his son and to make a career out of a lifelong love, Captain Fred began to invest in commercial fishing.

The investments are *big*. For fishermen like Captain Fred, one boat isn't enough. Today he owns three, including a twenty-five-foot NauticStar. It's a rod-and-reel trot line fishing boat that's good for sheepshead and black drum, Fred's main catches. A boat like this can cost as much as $80,000. And that is for a bay boat. An off-shore boat—required to fish in deep waters—can cost $1,000,000 if purchased new. Add to that another $10,000 to $15,000 in equipment—and that's on the low end. And you're legally required to have a commercial fishing license. A Texas Finfish Permit will run you $25,000 to $30,000. We're close to $300,000 now.

Access to money is a burden all commercial fishermen shoulder. But Black fishermen often face higher barriers, grounded in historic and contemporary restrictions of capital. They also confront racism and ignorance, on and off the water.

Captain Fred tells a story about a white fisherman who suggested to him that having such a nice boat meant that he was a drug dealer. Another time, he had a white mechanic working on his boat. A white fisherman whose boat was docked nearby spoke to the mechanic and refused to acknowledge Fred, assuming the white man must be the boat's owner. These incidents may seem slight, but when small aggressions accumulate, they feel like something big.

In the world of farming and agriculture, we've seen a huge resurgence of Black youth returning to the farmlands many of their ancestors left. From the 1950s onward, there was a dispossession of 98 percent of Black-owned land in America. Yet in recent years, many Black youth, knowledgeable to the legacy of farming pre-enslavement, have taken up farming. In doing so, they seek to heal the trauma of slavery and build ethical connections between Black communities and the land. Could it be that fishing has a place in this movement? Captain Fred hopes so. After all, as he sees it, the barriers to becoming a Black commercial fisherman are rooted in many of the same challenges—inequality, lack of access to capital, and lack of knowledge.

For Captain Fred, these challenges pale in comparison to the love he feels for the water. Over the last decade, he's built a successful business largely catching sheepshead for acclaimed Houston chefs. Chris Williams of Lucille's, Chris Shepherd of Underbelly Hospitality, and Jonny Rhodes of Broham Fine Soul Food and Groceries are all customers.

Captain Fred wants his business to provide opportunities for commercial fishermen who look like him, to help them open their own businesses and find peace along the water, just like his grandfather taught him. The effort is gaining strength.

Captain Fred has hopes to take kids out on his boat, similar to what his grandfather did with him. He plans to kick mentorship programs into gear in the coming years. Next year, Captain Fred plans to return to the school building. This time, not as a music teacher, but as a club leader, to build fishing clubs throughout the city. These clubs will teach fishing, lead field trips on the water, and offer true exposure to a new environment.

Fred McBride's life demonstrates the power of the water. And of Black people working the water. His story raises questions about who has access to the water and who profits from it. Stay tuned as he writes the answers.

KHADJIAH JOHNSON

Thanksgiving Is an RPG

FROM *Black Nerd Problems*

I REVELED IN their proclamations "Eh eh?!" My mother knows I just alley-ooped her when I came down the stairs with a platter. Eight apple roses, fresh from the oven, one for each guest. The looks started when I presented my family apple roses for Mother's Day dinner. A flashy, light, dessert with beams of red, and a scent that lit up the room. Cardamom, cinnamon, nutmeg, the aunties went wild.

If you want to be in the Thanksgiving lineup, you gotta make your goals clear. Because if you were not invited to the "entrees and sides" committee meeting, take your seat as the audience. Don't step foot in that kitchen during thanksgiving if you're not part of the support team. The Thanksgiving meeting is a sanctified chaos. The Thanksgiving meeting is where Black families lay the groundwork for the star-studded food lineup.

Bring out the Starting Lineup

First, we have the specialists; those are the aunties designated to the potato salad, or the person designated one dish and it's the same dish each year. The heavy hitters, those that handle the entrees and can serve as backup on the sides if there aren't enough reinforcements from the specialists. The ranged fighters; those on desserts. They aren't appreciated as much as they should be, but their sacrifices are well documented by the children. And finally, we have the healers, the blessed ones on the drinks. A couple sips rejuvenates the crowd for seconds. Not every Thanksgiving committee got a healer. Sometimes there are committee members who do this reluctantly or as an afterthought, but a well-crafted drink will get the spades/dominoes table hollering within minutes. The tryouts to get on the "sides and entrees" committee happens all year round. You will know when you get the call.

I need to plan out my method of attack. What am I aiming for? Heavy hitters show versatility. Specialists improve their dishes or got a solid recipe the family doesn't stray from. I want to be realistic, I don't have the appeal of a long-range fighter. I am notoriously anti-cake. And I watched enough cooking competitions to understand if you have never done something this intricate before, if you're doing it now, when the pressure is at 9,000?! You're asking for trouble.

A Frustrating Heavy Hitter

Prepping the Thanksgiving lineup feels reminiscent to the *MasterChef* team challenges. Contestants are split into reluctant teams of two and are placed in a pressure service. The contestants are sometimes asked to serve first responders, owners of famous restaurants, anything that would feel embarrassing to mess up. For the lineup, we have team leaders, wanna-be team leaders, the consistent support, and the chefs that fall behind. A notable heavy hitter that was frustrating to watch was Subha Ramiah.

For the entirety of *MasterChef* Season 10, I was angry at Subha. This man was lax in the kitchen. Time management? Terrible. Awareness? On three. But when he was on the bottom and had to pull out all the stops to save himself? His flavor? Supreme. Everyone was afraid to be matched with Subha in challenges, but in the same breath, they were afraid to be in the bottom with him because chances are, you were going home.

On episode 16 of season 10, the contestants were booked to serve NASCAR drivers. Set them plopped in the middle of the racetrack as they circle around them, loud noises and all. We're in the top 10 of the competition so the stakes are high, and any mess up can be critical. Subha is on the red team, with Micah as the team captain. It seems that Micah's biggest issue is managing Subha because somehow Subha burns the chicken. But the plot twist is, Subha was not originally assigned to the meat station. He charred it. The kind of char that makes the top of the skin look like a NASCAR tire.

So, when Micah's team wins and is given an advantage to put one of his team members up for elimination, he doesn't pick the front-runner Dorian; he picks Subha. Subha came out of that elimination challenge unscathed, but Thanksgiving potlucks run similar to this: If you don't come consistent you will be thrown under the bus at the meeting.

Weakness in the Structure

In RPGs, I am either one of two characters: the first line of attack, going head first into battle, or the micro-managing healer making sure no one's health drops below 60%. I know I got heavy hitter capabilities, but that requires me to go into the Thanksgiving lineup with a plan. My first thought? Look for weaknesses in the structure.

There are a couple of dishes I think could be much better. But pointing this out can come at the expense of people's egos. I already got a few culprits in mind because I see the stats. When the to-go containers come out, whose dishes are in immediate danger? The person that be bringing the potato salad? They been lacking ever since they put the green peas in there. The person that prepares the chicken? Those legs been overcooked for three straight holidays. I can offer myself as tribute, throw in an improvement, but Thanksgiving lineups hide behind the veil of respectability politics. If you don't come out the doors with stats, your argument for improvement does not suffice. If you don't have enough "guts" character stats to say, "putting BBQ sauce on that leg not gonna make the chicken any less Sahara"; and then pop out with the juiciest jerk chicken alive? You'll be banished from future consideration if you don't come correct.

Or maybe I can bring something new to the table. The safe way to not piss anybody off. But being a team sport is arguably much harder. Not only do you have to bring something new, it has to be fire enough where people want to get it more than once. If I notice we have a lot of decadent dishes, maybe I can craft something light to balance the plate.

Shokugeki No Soma Taught Me Nothing But Violence

Like Thanksgiving, *Food Wars!* taught me nothing but violence. You prove your place with flavor. Respectability politics in the Afro-Caribbean household always made me cringe. If someone normally makes this dish, even if it's bad and we have ways of improving, they must keep making this dish. They know best because they have been doing it for so long. Respecting culture is different than adhering to hierarchy. In episode 45 of *Shokugeki No Soma*, the food clubs are under fire. They must throw out their innovations and practices in order to adhere to the new director's food manual. Everyone must only make a certain type of dish and made in a specific way. Students disassociating from this manual will be expelled.

Innovation was frowned upon while classism had taken its hold. In order to save his dorm, protagonist Soma Yukihira challenged Chef Eizan "The Alchemist" seat number seven in the Council of Ten to a food war. With a board of judges willing to forgo tasting a dish because it uses ingredients not considered "top quality" or doesn't put the quality of an ingredient above its preparation, it goes completely against Soma Yukihira's style. Soma utilizes every day's cheap delights and elevating it into deliciousness. Chef Eizan presented Khao Man Gai, taking careful attention to not alter the chicken's natural flavors too much. One bite and every tongue squealed with bliss. Eizan presented a formidable classic that didn't stray too far from the books.

Season of the Underdog

Soma Yukihira was the underdog. The judges were prepared to discard his dish and name Soma defeated without taking a bite. Soma prepared a chicken wing gyoza with a rich ankake sauce. He removed the bones of the chicken and stuffed the cavity with ground pork, shiitake mushrooms, scallions and cabbage, then prepared a bone broth and used it to make the ankake sauce. From the jump, I was like oh shit, that's fire. Captivated by the scent, a judge took a bite. He was taken aback by the flavor! The delight. Soma Yukihira won the food war and saved his dorm.

In *Shokugeki No Soma*, you can tell how delicious food is due to the sudden unraveling of clothes. A character takes a bite and is immediately transported into a haven where they're doused in sauce and relishing in spices. Food wars, where the food is so delicious, threads are no longer worthy of people's body. I aspire to such deliciousness, but Thanksgiving is a place where I look for cracks in a foundation . . . it's where I find my place. I got it. Appetizers. People are always waiting hours for food. Sometimes, the kitchen is not done until 6pm, but there's people with kids and you know what people can't get enough of? Wings.

If All Else Fails, Wing It!

I realized this might be the passive aggressive way of knocking out the other heavy hitter that brings in the jerk chicken every year. I got enough exp points to throw hands if I must. I marinated the wings in a berbere overnight with a slight pinch of baking powder. Baking powder dehydrates the skin and allows it to crisp in the oven.

Round one. Crispy berbere wings served with a lemon thyme yogurt sauce. The spice for the heat lovers, served with a cooling agent for those on the less daring side. 30+ hit damage. Brought it out on one of those appetizer towers you see at tea shops. 40+ hit damage. The aunties are scrambling. The visuals kept them coming. What were they going to argue about? If anything, I saved them time and alley-ooped my mother once again. +20 hit damage. The final boss is down, but you have to keep rolling. I pulled out three rounds of fresh wings. One after the other. People got off the cooks' backs and stayed out of the kitchen. The kids, no longer screaming. I have won. I have secured my spot in the heavy hitter's ceremony in my 20s by creating a wave of delicious convenience.

I realized this when my grandmother started calling me for cooking advice. Or last week when my mother tried to convince me to fly down and prepare a platter. *Food became all about experimentation and bringing smiles to the people I loved and indulging in cultures I couldn't when I was a kid.* My Thanksgiving prep is never complete if I'm not returning to Tōtsuki Culinary Academy or cringing at kitchen mistakes in culinary competitions. Always returning to my roots, because if I must, I'm willing to sheathe knives.

LYNDSAY C. GREEN

Effortless Anonymity

FROM *Detroit Free Press*

THERE WERE TWO outcomes of my job interview with *Detroit Free Press* editor and vice president Peter Bhatia. The most obvious, my appointment as the paper's restaurant critic, the second, a running joke. Sitting across from me at a table at a Starbucks in downtown Detroit, Peter inquired about my thoughts on anonymity in restaurant criticism. "I'm 4–10, Black, and I have platinum blond hair," I said to my potential future employer with a smirk. Months in quarantine seemed a safe enough time for my first major hair color experiment, but as I eased back into social settings, the hair became tricky to hide. "It'd be quite difficult to remain anonymous for long."

It was a risk, bringing up race in an interview—albeit stating the obvious. It was also a risk to challenge the tradition of anonymity at a paper that has prided itself on editorial integrity for more than a century.

Anonymity allows a writer to step into a restaurant without risking an outing where the staff panders to their position of power to make or break the place. (James Beard Award–winning chef and author Joseph "JJ" Johnson once told *New York Magazine*'s Grub Street that sales increased by 80% when a critic reviewed his former Harlem restaurant The Cecil. And reservations for nearly all restaurants on the *Free Press*'s 2022 10 Best New Restaurants list were booked for weeks after the winners were announced.)

When restaurant critics conceal their identities, they ensure the sincerity of a dining experience. Not long ago, Sylvia Rector, the late critic who reimagined restaurant criticism at the *Free Press*, just barely bared her brown eyes through the tines of a silver fork in her column headshot.

Peter, whose raspy voice up until that point had been fairly quiet—serious even—let out a hearty laugh. He agreed with the sentiment and added that the paper had shed its traditional approach to anonymity in recent years. The *Free Press* was entering a progressive era that welcomes columnists and critics to have a more outward-facing presence. If I were to get the job, I'd still be expected to assume a level of discretion, but aliases and disguises would not be necessary.

The next time we spoke, Peter told me that he'd shared my quip with his wife. As a petite woman, she related to the self-deprecating nudge at my short stature. And during my first staff meeting at the Freep HQ, Peter asked for approval to let the newsroom in on the joke before introducing me as one of the newest members to the team. By then, my platinum blond hair had faded, clinging only to my split ends like the frosted-tips trend of the early 2000s. But the curly afro that hovered over me like a halo ensured my hair would forever be one of my most distinguishing features.

The joke became a welcome ice breaker my first week on the job.

I've since learned that what was even more laughable, though, was the idea that my most recognizable features would make me memorable at all. Over the next year as the *Free Press*'s dining and restaurant critic, I'd discover that despite my big hair and tellingly short stature, my brown skin color and oversized round glasses, my penchant for red lipstick and elaborate outfits, I'd find myself entirely incognito in the costume of my own skin.

What may have been a welcome perk for the anonymous critics of yore, has instead hinted at something deeper about how America—and especially its upscale dining spheres—views Black women.

Now Serving Dessert

As the title suggests, my role as dining and restaurant critic is a hybrid—I'm part private eye of restaurants and translator of taste, part reporter on metro Detroit's dining scene. It's a split-personality of sorts, one in which I am expected to maintain a low profile to ensure the dining experience of a common diner, and another where I am an industry insider, privy to restaurant and food news before it reaches the common diner. When looking to the gold standard of each of my roles, there's an instinct to be as renowned as food writers who have risen to Food Network acclaim and yet as inconspicuous as the critics whose photos have been scrubbed from the Internet.

It's a tightrope act to get a restauranteur to offer an exclusive tip or a hard-hat first glimpse of their next restaurant opening, only to slip in months later to review that same restaurant undetected. An unintentional master of disguise with a superpower of invisibility though, the latter has been easy enough.

As curator of the annual *Detroit Free Press* Restaurant of the Year and Top 10 Best New Restaurants list, it is my responsibility to name the city's most accomplished new restaurants. And as host of the paper's Top 10 Takeover, the dinner series that trails the unveiling of the list, I recite a brief speech that recaps the reasons each restaurant earned its respective spot on the coveted list and present an award to the honored chef at the helm.

In most cases, I've likely interacted with the winning chef at least twice at the time of the dinner series—once for background information and again for an official interview. Then there are the mutual follows on social media. We've double-tapped photos taken with our spouses and reacted to images shared of our latest meals.

That's what makes what happens next so mystifying.

It's not my ego or the expectation that my face is plastered on the kitchen as in the case of critics in big coastal cities like New York and Los Angeles, but rather genuine shock during a recent visit to one of the Top 10 Best New Restaurants when the executive chef brings a plate of dessert to my table without recognizing my face. That evening, without my recorder or an award in hand, I was just another diner. The chef happily ran down the noteworthy ingredients and the garnishes on the creamy frozen treat as I searched his eyes for a glimmer of recognition.

It was dim at the restaurant. He must not have seen my face clearly.

"Who Are You With?"
With my short stature and polite instinct to take up as little space as possible, I've used my smallness to my advantage. In grade school, the petite, well-mannered, quiet girl could never be capable of wrongdoing. In crowds, it's easy enough to zig-zag through the gaps between bodies like a marble on a wooden maze board.

And as a restaurant critic, even in a post-anonymous era, being unrecognizable is acceptable—in many ways, preferred.

As a human being, feeling invisible is an entirely new insult.

My obscurity goes beyond my days as a restaurant critic. It goes back to my time as a beauty editor on New York City's women's magazine scene, when it felt as though I didn't fit in or stand out, but rather as though I was cast aside for the taller, thinner, whiter, more personable, more confident caste. The type who was more likely to climb the ranks and therefore, more worthy of schmoozing.

Backstage during New York Fashion Week, I chatted at length with a publicist. We might have even exchanged phone numbers, advancing to a new level of professional familiarity. The next day, I'd arrived at the same tent excited to see my newfound friend. She would surely forgive my running a few minutes behind and quietly usher me backstage.

"Who are you with?" she asked, stone-faced.

She searched the list of VIPs on the clipboard she was clutching for the name and publication associated with the person standing before her. I must not have looked very important.

As hurt as I was, and as small as I felt, I found myself comforting *her* after clumsily uttering my name. I quickly forgave her for forgetting me.

My hair was different that day. Why should she have recognized me?

My obscurity is indiscriminate. I can slip into ambiguity no matter the race of the person I'm interacting with. There was the swanky press trip to Barcelona, where I bonded with a fellow writer over glasses of Spanish red wine. At an event stateside a week later, she brushed past me gingerly, apologizing for stepping on my toes as she looked for her seat a few chairs down the row. No matter how hard I smiled or tried to catch her attention, she never recognized my face.

Was it that much wine? I tried to recall.

The feeling of familiarity has become increasingly foreign. Where most people expect a fondness, a smile of recognition when you see a face you know, I've grown to expect something far less welcoming. That awkward dart of a person's eyes when they're trying to evade mine, the clear look of someone desperately trying to recall why I'd dare know their name, or that tight-lipped smirk reserved only for strangers when you're trying to be polite. Then, there's the eventual blush of embarrassment that comes once I've jogged a person's memory.

There are the countless times co-workers have reintroduced themselves if I've straightened my hair or slicked it into a bun. Or the times I've had to reintroduce myself to a chef I've interviewed various times when ordering takeout at their restaurant. I've learned to skip the reminder altogether and pass like a ship in the night. It's less awkward for both of us that way.

Sitting at the bright and airy James Oliver Coffee Co. writing this very story, I've had to jog the memory of two diners—one, a man I'd met only recently at a dinner party, another, a fellow food writer who I'd consider a friend. Both with the same response after what felt like me jumping up and down and waving my hands in the air as if to say, "It's me! Can't you see me?" At the dinner party, he'd been kind to me, and she and I had texted just days before. At the coffee shop, between bites of vegan chili and sips of frothy red eyes, neither of them had a clue who I was. There was also a Best New Restaurant owner who I didn't bother trying to flag down.

Missus Cellophane should've been my name.

Who Do You Think You Are?

I'd held out as long as I could before publishing my first less-than-savory review of a restaurant.

I considered all that restaurant owners were burdened with as the pandemic entered into a new phase of perpetual trauma. Ultimately, I'd decided the pandemic pendulum swings both ways. Just as restaurants are facing unchartered challenges, diners, too are making great sacrifices to eat out. The least I could do was share an honest account when a restaurant didn't live up to its fine dining expectations.

The review was shared and re-shared, picked up and picked apart, but no one hated the piece more than the restaurant's owner.

She knew enough about me to track down my email, but not enough to shame me effectively. She copied the editor of the paper—it wasn't the right paper. Even via email, I'd been so unmemorable, she didn't have the capacity to remember the publication in which she'd read my work.

"Instead of reaching out to us, and maybe getting a little insight into what is really happening in the restaurant business, you just decide to write a very snarky review of our restaurant," she wrote.

Coincidentally, I *had* sat down with her.

A few months prior, we sat at an intimate table in the empty restaurant, joined only by her husband and their publicist. We spoke at length for more than an hour over coffee to discuss the many challenges the duo faced as restaurant operators in metro Detroit.

We didn't sit down to talk for this story, per se. I was at a different outlet at the time. She must know I'm the same girl—right?

"Nobody Notices Old Ladies"

In her memoir *Garlic and Sapphires: The Secret Life of a Critic in Disguise*, (Penguin Books, 2005), former *New York Times* restaurant critic and University of Michigan alum Ruth Reichl quoted a friend saying, "Nobody notices old ladies," as she attempted to convince Reichl to disguise herself as her late mother for their next restaurant outing. Reichl's costumes were dual-purposed, mainly to conceal her identity during her time as restaurant critic at the *Times*, but also to provide insight on how her appearance influenced the way restaurant staffers would treat—or disregard her.

Today, I am the *Detroit Free Press*'s first Black restaurant critic, and it appears, one of few, if not the only Black restaurant critic at a major newspaper in the country. What does not being noticed say when you're a Black woman—a majority in the city you report on, but a minority in Detroit's fine dining spaces? Could it be that my superpower of being invisible when crossing the threshold of a dining space is perhaps more sinister when examined with more scrutiny?

In a 2019 *Eater* essay, Korsha Wilson illuminated a missing perspective in restaurant criticism: the perspective of a Black diner. At the time of the article, it seemed there had never been a Black restaurant critic at a major publication apart from culinary historian Jessica Harris, who contributed reviews at the *Village Voice* in the late '90s into the early 2000s. Nearly four years later, little progress has been made.

This brings to mind the more unnerving instances when I *have* been noticed. Like the time I was asked whether I belonged at a ritzy private dinner held for food writers and other members of the media, or when a woman asked if I was filling in for the restaurant critic who was *supposed* to give a library talk.

It couldn't possibly be me who belonged in these spaces.

In some ways, it's a comical story. The makings of a thrilling sci-fi about how I magically disappear in plain sight when entering a restaurant. But upon further reflection, perhaps this story is as much a horror as the nonfiction accounts of invisible Black women in everyday life.

Yes, I'm 4-foot-10, Black, and my naturally curly hair is larger than life. But anonymity is a choice. My invisibility is inevitable.

LIGAYA MISHAN

What We Write About When We Write About Food

FROM *T: The New York Times Style Magazine*

"TELL ME, MUSE, of the dinners, much-nourishing and many in number." So wrote the Greek poet Matro of Pitane in the fourth century BC, stealing the exalted opening of the *Odyssey* ("Tell me, Muse, of the man of many ways") for his "Convivium Atticum" and memorializing in epic hexameter a tale in which there are no heroes, only eaters, and no perils to overcome, just food upon food, in mocking homage to the *Iliad*'s catalog of ships massed for Troy: loaves "whiter than snow"; 13 "very fat" ducks; an eel the length of nine tables; and so many fish and of such kind and season as would have been impossible to serve all at once. The only suffering is a distended stomach.

To the Greeks, or at least those aristocratic enough to qualify as Matro's audience, this was parody. Food, as the subject of poetry, was ridiculous. The desire for it, beyond what was needed to survive, spoke to baser instincts. (Philosophers distinguished in a meal between *sitos*, the staple, and *opson*, the relish, and warned against overly prizing the latter.) To care too much about what you ate made you a glutton, an epithet applied to another poet of the fourth century BC, Archestratos of Gela, who braved the seas in pursuit of local specialties, a proto-Anthony Bourdain. "To hell with saperde"—a kind of cured fish—"And those who praise it," he grouses in his gastronomic litany the *Hedypatheia*, of which only fragments survive. He denounces tiny fish as no better than excrement, save for the finer specimens caught in the waters off

Athens, and offers, as cooking instructions, a brusque "Don't burn it up."

Yet this voice of more than two millenniums ago is uncannily recognizable to readers of today: declarative, hyperbolic, gossipy and confiding, faintly aggrieved, assuming, perhaps unearned, a mantle of authority and even omniscience ("Few people know which food is wretched and which is excellent"), giving freight to the smallest bite, finding rapture in what sates. In short, Archestratos was a food writer. Or so we might label him now, as kin to those specialists of our own time, the literary-minded cooks who know that every recipe comes with a story; the memoirists who recall each meal as half debauchery, half revelation; the journalists who stake out tailgates and backyard barbecues; and the critics who skulk into restaurants in disguise, brandishing words like knives.

But what separates a food writer from someone who just happens to write about food? As with any compartmentalizing of genre, there is something in the title that implies a diminishment, as if today, as in ancient Greece, the act of eating were too frivolous to be worthy of serious meditation. Matro aimed for comedy in the excesses of his dinner-party verse, but the tone of Archestratos' work isn't so clear, and he was disdained by later scholars for daring to imagine that, in compiling an index of culinary pleasures, he was "laying the foundation of some science likely to improve human existence." Still, when contemporary food writers (and, I suppose, I am one) stray from celebrating flavors to probe the larger issues surrounding the parade of dishes to our tables—exploitation of labor, abuse of animals, climate change, the homogenizing of cuisines and cultures under globalization, systemic injustices that allow millions of people to go hungry each year—some readers complain. Food should not be political, they insist. Food is universal; food unites us. Let us have our cake in peace.

Of course, people have always written about food. Our earliest surviving recipes were carved into tablets in Mesopotamia nearly 4,000 years ago; a text from the same millennium includes a spoof menu of seasonal dishes featuring ingredients like donkey haunch and the excrement of dogs and dust flies. (Scatological humor is evidently equally eternal.) The Greek historian Herodotus, in the fifth century BC, minutely documented the foodways of "barbarian" (i.e., non-Greek) cultures, mostly from information that was obtained secondhand and sometimes fantastical—he observes that the Persians pile on desserts, while the Scythians drink horse milk and prefer their food boiled—and it remains a question whether this was intended to make these foreigners seem more alien, and thus inferior to the Greeks, or to show, through the common act of eating, how much people are the same.

A literature dedicated to food, however, beyond manuals on the technicalities of cooking, is of more recent vintage. In Paris in the mid-18th century, there emerged the peculiar institution known today as the restaurant—originally, the word signified the kind of restorative consommé served at such places—which yielded, in the early 19th century, the first restaurant critic, Alexandre-Balthazar-Laurent Grimod de La Reynière, who published culinary guidebooks and a monthly journal for which he convened friends to sit in judgment on the city's chefs. The epicure Jean Anthelme Brillat-Savarin's weighty *The Physiology of Taste* (1825) elevated eating to a discipline for historians and philosophers, a tradition furthered in the 20th century in the West by writers who made cookbooks meant to be read, not just followed, and who changed the way people and even entire nations ate and thought about food, from Elizabeth David and Claudia Roden in England to Edna Lewis and Madhur Jaffrey in the United States. Today, there is so much written about food, in so many forms and outlets, that it can be difficult to define as a coherent genre.

It's notable, then, that "food writer" did not come into American usage until the 1930s, and it was a specifically professional term. Proliferating food corporations sought to woo customers by publishing cunning pamphlets in which snippets of poems and quotes from 19th-century luminaries such as Brillat-Savarin and the British Prime Minister Benjamin Disraeli—"The most delicious thing in the world is a banana," he wrote to his sister in 1831 while sojourning in Cairo—appeared embedded alongside recipes for the likes of heart-shaped Wonder Bread "honeymoon" sandwiches and cocktail glasses filled with California canned asparagus tips and tomato aspic, served "very cold." The targets of such advertising, and often the writers of it, were women, who at the time were responsible for running the household. (In 1932, *National Business*

Woman magazine fielded queries from readers as to "what courses in home economics ought I to take to become a food writer?") Even in journalism, food was viewed as a domestic matter and limited to what were called, dismissively, the women's pages.

Then, kitchens changed. In 1920, a little more than a third of American homes were equipped with electricity, but by 1930, that number had nearly doubled, and the widespread adoption of modern appliances—gas and electric stovetops in the 1920s, refrigerators in the 1930s—alleviated the hardship of preparing meals. This made it possible to view cooking as a leisure activity and an opportunity to show off, and that's when husbands began to muscle in. The mainstream media took notice. In 1940, *Esquire* launched a food column touting the superiority of masculine taste, "Man the Kitchenette." (Never mind that the author, Iles Brody, had gained notoriety for reportedly beating his girlfriends and attempting blackmail.) Two years later, the *New York Times* deputized its first food editor, Jane Nickerson. She was the first to use the term "food writer" in its pages, although she also drolly (and perhaps bitingly) referred to members of her profession as "the palate press" in a 1949 report on an haute cruise-ship meal of braised celery hearts and Dom Pérignon, presented by a male chef who proclaimed that "the art of cooking is like a beautiful woman—indescribable," which may have left his audience wondering why they'd been invited to describe it in the first place.

By the 1970s, newspapers across the country were churning out stand-alone food sections, staffed mostly by women. Their work was popular but not respected, and was suspected of existing only to promote the products of food companies whose ads kept the newspapers afloat. Eventually, these food writers drew the ire of Senator Frank Moss, Democrat of Utah, a champion of consumers' rights, as chronicled by Kimberly Wilmot Voss in *The Food Section: Newspaper Women and the Culinary Community* (2014). In 1971, invited to speak at the National Conference of Food Editors in Chicago, Moss baldly asked the assembly, "Ladies, are you the pawns of your advertising managers . . . or are you journalists?," and then branded them "whores of the supermarket industry."

The women hissed. Some walked out. A group of them would go on to form their own professional organization and draft a strict code of ethics to stave off further accusations. Although Moss railed about opening a Senate investigation, nothing happened.

(As Voss points out, there was the problem of the First Amendment, after all.) Meanwhile, the editors in chief and owners of the newspapers and magazines the women worked for, who determined the scope of their stories and were predominantly male, went blithely on their way, never called to account.

Consumerism is a "revolt against the unresponsiveness of government and industry to the crying needs of the public," Moss told Congress in 1971. He was an idealist, however bungled this particular episode in his crusade. Half a century later, consumerism has triumphed, although not in the sense that Moss understood it, as fighting on behalf of consumers against unfair business practices, but in the pejorative form of a society that privileges the consumption of goods above all, even above the rights of the workers who make them. Notably, "food writer" didn't truly enter the American vernacular until the early 21st century in the wake of *Kitchen Confidential* (2000), Bourdain's coruscating behind-the-scenes exposé of his own life as a chef running a restaurant. Although the book was in part a testament to the unseen labor that goes into every dish, the main takeaway for many readers was Bourdain's advice never to order fish on a Monday (because it may be left over from a Friday delivery). They identified with the customers— rather like readers of Upton Sinclair's 1906 social-realist novel, *The Jungle*, who were more outraged by the prospect of tainted food on their plates than by meat packers forced to work in filthy and dangerous conditions.

We don't mind product promotion now, although we still don't like the idea of writers being bribed to do it; we want to believe we're being urged to buy things because they really are that good— because we *like* to buy things. The food writer Molly O'Neill noted in 2003 that the people who bought the most expensive kitchen appliances tended to cook the least, transforming cooking into a "spectator sport." Food writing, in turn, had devolved into food porn. "There is a place in newspaper food sections and food magazines for cheery, revisionist, nostalgic waxings; for songs of dew-kissed baby lettuces; for Proustian glances back," she writes. "But there is a line between soothing readers' anxieties and becoming the Victoria's Secret of the Fourth Estate."

How can food writing soothe readers when food itself is the locus of so much social anxiety? This is the hidden thread that

runs through food writing from the ancients to today that threatens
to pull and unravel. The British social anthropologist Jack Goody
has argued that the advent of cuisine as we know it—as opposed to
the food eaten by everyone in a particular community—is predi-
cated on inequality: When one group gains control of a larger share
of resources and access to ingredients from other regions, making
and eating food of increased variety and complexity become a
way to mark status. Going further, the British sociologist Stephen
Mennell has suggested that the extreme stratification of society
is insufficient, yielding only differences in quantity, not quality of
food; what drives culinary innovation is rather the emergence of
closer-knit, competitive classes jockeying for power, with those on
lower rungs exerting "pressure from below."

So when we write about food, we are already writing about class
struggle. "The cooking of a society is a language in which it un-
consciously translates its structure," the French anthropologist
Claude Lévi-Strauss wrote in 1966. To read about an extravagant
meal can be a vicarious substitute for not being able to afford
one or make us feel superior to those who waste their money on
such follies. We especially love tales of astronomically priced meals
gone wrong, from the *Times* critic Pete Wells's calm, lucid evis-
ceration in 2015 of the "brutally, illogically, relentlessly" expensive Japanese restaurant Kappo Masa on Manhattan's Upper East
Side—"A pantomime of service . . . an imitation of luxury"—to the
travel blogger Geraldine DeRuiter's viral takedown last December
of the Michelin-starred Bros', in Lecce, Italy, in which 27 courses
were served, consisting mainly of "slivers of edible paper," "glasses
of vinegar," and "12 kinds of foam," including one sprayed into a
plaster cast of the chef's mouth and drooling down one side, for
the diner to lap up with her tongue. Such stories confirm that the
emperor has no clothes; that we're not missing a thing.

In the *Hedypatheia*, Archestratos mentions silphium, a wild herb
believed to be akin to asafetida and since lost to history. The plant
was so coveted it was overforaged, and by the first century AD,
according to the Roman historian Pliny the Elder, only "a single
stalk" could be found; Archestratos was its elegist in advance without
knowing it. What we gain in the complexity of cuisine inevitably has
a cost in labor and on the environment. Maybe the nostalgia that
O'Neill fears is the default for contemporary food writing is, in fact,

nostalgia for the present, which is slipping ever more quickly into the past, and even nostalgia for the future, one we may never have.

MFK Fisher, arguably the greatest American food writer, if not one of the greatest writers across the board, was exquisitely nostalgic, but she had wickedness, too. When she published her first collection of essays on food, *Serve It Forth*, in 1937, the *Times* deemed it "delightful" but the material "unfamiliar and odd." To this day, she eludes categorization; to say that she wrote about food is like saying that Virginia Woolf and James Joyce wrote about dinner parties. In *The Gastronomical Me* (1943), she recalls the banality of childhood meals under the iron glare of her grandmother, who, along with "unhappy millions of Anglo-Saxons," had been schooled in the principle "that food should be consumed without comment of any kind but above all without sign of praise or enjoyment." A new cook comes in for a few weeks and the results are baffling and thrilling, leaving Fisher in "a kind of anguish of delight." Then, one evening, the cook doesn't return, and it turns out that she has killed her mother and herself, with the very knife she'd wielded so expertly in the kitchen.

It's a gruesome twist, but this does not dim the cook's aura in Fisher's eyes. She mourns but retains the "consciousness of the possibilities of the table" and grows up to be herself the kind of cook— and writer—determined to shake people "from their routines, not only of meat-potatoes-gravy but of thought, of behavior." And, more forcefully: "To blast their safe, tidy little lives." Surely there is no better mantra for a food writer today, wallowing in scraps and swinging for the stars. What more could we give our readers? For what is the point of reading about food or, for that matter, reading about anything at all: to look in a mirror, or through a window; to escape the world, or to discover it?

MADHUSHREE GHOSH

On the Road, a Taste of Home

FROM *High Country News*

WALKING INTO PUNJABI Tandoor, located in a strip mall in Carlsbad, about 25 miles north of San Diego, I'm struck by the contrast between the harsh fluorescent lights and the delightful fragrance of garam masala, onions, and garlic. The owners already know what I want, ladling my favorite three-item combo into a Styrofoam container of curries heaped over fragrant jasmine rice. They pile on generous dollops of cauliflower and saag paneer. I dig into this quintessential North Indian fare, the taste immediately reminding me of home.

Punjabi Tandoor, run by Bakhtawar Saini and his cousin, Jagdish, caters to Indian immigrants in Southern California, people working in software or biotech, like me, or studying at nearby colleges. Eateries like this have sprung up all over California, in strip malls, business parks, and along the freeway rest stops where the old burger joints once reigned supreme. They serve the growing ranks of Sikh long-haul truckers who move produce, fruits, nuts, and dry goods from California's rich agricultural lands to the rest of the country and beyond.

These establishments offer more than comfort food and a taste of home cooking. They also provide reassurance that while their patrons may be far from home, the food along the freeways exists to remind them of the way back.

Jagdish mans the large clay tandoor oven while his daughters take people's orders and run the register. Two decades ago, on my first visit to their Mira Mar restaurant, I had asked Jagdish Saini about an Indian restaurant on Black Mountain Road. The restaurant served mediocre food, but he replied respectfully, "I want them to succeed."

A religious Sikh, Jagdish isn't interested in badmouthing his competition. Rather, he's focused on what Indians term *atithi devo bhava*, or "the guest is God" philosophy. His customers, he says, bring him closer to divinity.

Bakhtawar has now opened multiple restaurants, and I've been a regular customer at all of them.

What diners and dives are to California freeways, Punjabi dhabas are to Indian highways. Growing up in Delhi, I was used to the dhabas lining our roads. Tiny ramshackle stalls with roaring burners, a fired-up clay tandoor, and perennially boiling milk tea on a separate burner: This was what late-night expeditions were about. Dhabas were not only for truckers and long-haul drivers, but also for college students, party-goers, travelers, and anyone who needed a break, a chai, hot food and a place to rest. Typical dhaba fare includes bright chicken masala curry, thin rotis, paneer tikka, thick choley curry or spinach aloo alongside clay glasses of ginger chai. In India, it was comfort food; more than that, it was food that marked when we became adults, and our parents allowed us to drive long distances. At the dhabas, we were treated as grownups, making new friends and then moving away. The highways and rest stops and dhabas highlighted the newfound freedom of our generation.

Sikh Punjabi agricultural workers brought the dhaba tradition with them when they came to California in the late 19th and early 20th centuries. They were met with systematic discrimination in the form of anti-miscegenation laws and state land acts that denied immigrants citizenship grants and the chance to own land. The men were unable to bring their families from India, and so many married Mexican farmworkers, creating a hybrid community of about 2,000 people in the Bakersfield and the Yuba-Sutter areas. In response, local restaurants began melding Punjabi and Mexican cuisine, creating new dishes like the roti quesadilla and lamb burrito. The next wave of immigrants from Punjab came after the passage of the 1965 Immigration and Nationality Act. This time, entire Sikh families migrated, creating a "mini Punjab" with schools, gurudwaras, and community centers in various California communities.

Sikhism, which began in the 15th century, differed from the

Hinduism and Islam that then prevailed in India; they accepted other religions and the equality of men and women, reflected in similar names, and they celebrated Guru Granth Sahib and the holy texts instead of idols. Sikhs have long been known as brave warriors who are also people of peace and faith, but they often faced persecution in India. Finally, in the 1980s, Jarnail Singh Bhindranwale led an uprising and took over northern India, demanding a separate nation and the freedom to practice their religion. Faced with retaliation by the Indian armed forces, Bhindranwale and his followers took refuge in the Sikh house of worship in Amritsar, the Golden Temple. The Indian military stormed the temple in what became known as Operation Bluestar, killing Bhindranwale along with many of his followers and thousands of civilians who had come to the temple to pray. Trauma reverberated through the decades that followed.

Four months after the storming of the Golden Temple, Prime Minister Indira Gandhi was assassinated by her Sikh bodyguards. This prompted even harsher reprisals: Over 2,800 Sikhs were killed in Delhi during just a few days, and at least 50,000 Sikhs were displaced from New Delhi and adjoining areas. The 1984 massacre sparked a mass migration of Sikhs from India to Canada, the U.S., and England. Sikh communities in the U.S. grew, and many Sikhs became truckers in California and the West. Before long, Punjabi dhabas were sprouting up at the rest stops along the I-10, I-5, and I-40 freeways.

Punjabi Tandoor has three branches in San Diego: the closet-sized one in Mira Mar I frequented whenever I was homesick; a second one in a former sushi restaurant near Sorrento Valley; and a third one in Carlsbad, north of San Diego, in a strip mall across from biotech behemoths bustling with afternoon lunch traffic.

Jagdish's daughter, Satwinder, leads the cash register in the Carlsbad restaurant with a perpetual smile and an Americanized accent. Much like her family, she spends her free time at the San Diego gurudwara, since prayer and service are an important part of her life. Lucky, her cousin, a tall skinny young man with a thick Sikh turban and even thicker black beard, handles the tandoor, sticking the naan on the side of the hot oven and keeping an eye on the boiling chicken curry handi. Throughout the day, he fields customers' questions about how spicy a "level seven" might be, or whether the navratan korma is a better choice than the choley today.

On the restaurant television mounted on the wall, European football or cricket plays on mute. This is "desi timepass," as we call it—sports, food, and family.

Satwinder fills up a container with lamb curry; the spices mixed with the creamy yogurt remind me of home every time. Lucky makes me a roti because I prefer it to naan. Jagdish quietly boils the tea; no Indian will say no to an offer of chai.

The food is always the same, as is the service. And always, I am treated as family.

Bakhtawar Saini doesn't talk about what it was like when he first came to California, back in the 1980s. Shrugging, he asks instead, "Have you tried food in all our restaurants?"

"Yes," I reply. "Same menu, no?"

"That's the idea. Whether you eat it in Carlsbad or Mira Mesa, the food tastes like from Punjab. Quality is what we look for."

He adds, "It brings you back home. I've visited Italy, Germany, England—now here. I ate Punjabi food everywhere. The flavor's the same."

He isn't talking about fancy gourmet cooking, but about the pure delight of comfort food. It's the familiar smell that makes you want that saag paneer, returning you to your childhood. When you eat at Punjabi Tandoor, you belong.

"Come again," he says, inviting me back formally.

Later, I ask Lucky why Bakhtawar wouldn't talk about the riots, Lucky shrugs, smiling, "Arre, it was so long ago," he says. "I wasn't even born. We focus on good—hard work, honesty. And the rest— *baaki, rab jaane.*"

The rest, God will take care.

The head-down, model-immigrant trope continues, even though the individual stories remain untold. The Sainis and their Punjabi restaurants in America's Finest City bring me that much closer to a conflict-ridden land I left three decades ago.

At the Mira Mesa Punjabi Tandoor register, a sign advertises a summer special on rose milk. It is also a celebration of Sikhism. A small sign below it proclaims, "Good vibes only."

In 1983, a year before the Sikh temple desecration, before Indira Gandhi was assassinated, before thousands of Sikhs were killed, before the family fled India, I sat in a hot and humid taxi next to Jagat Sudhar Gurudwara in Kolkata, the city my parents came from, a city we visited every summer to be with our cousins and extended family.

A Sikh boy—his hair in a tight topknot covered with a small handkerchief—knocked at the taxi's window. "Dada, brother, yeh lo!"

The driver reached for a glass filled with a pink lassi-like sherbet. Baba asked, "How much?"

"Nah, no money, sir," the boy laughed, "it's Guru Arjan's shaheedi, we celebrate with chabeel, kachi lassi. We feed the hungry, and the thirsty. Want a glass?"

My father accepted the glass. Ma hesitated; unfiltered water can lead to upset stomachs, but Baba chugged his drink down.

"Baah," he said, in appreciation, "that was refreshing! Rose, yogurt, so nice."

The boy took the glass back, yelling, "*Sat sri akal!*" Glory be to God.

The drink, we later learned, brings respite to weary travelers even as it honors the Arjan's martyrdom, remembering the guru who was executed by the Muslim emperor. He had asked his Sikh followers to defend their religion and live with dignity and honesty—a martyred guru who is celebrated with optimism by his followers, centuries later.

Baba's stomach held fine. Behind us, the Sikh boy held up glasses of rose milk, spreading happiness.

For those of us who still miss home, a small Punjabi restaurant in Southern California run by a long-persecuted people is the closest thing to being there.

Good vibes only.

MARION NESTLE

Regulating the Food Industry: An Aspirational Agenda

FROM *American Journal of Public Health*

THE CORONAVIRUS PANDEMIC reveals an urgent need: the marketing of ultra-processed "junk" food must be stopped. Until now, the food industry has gotten away with pushing consumption of high-calorie, highly processed products—as often and in as many places as possible, and in increasingly large amounts—all in the name of profit. In this business-first food environment, obesity and its associated type 2 diabetes, coronary heart disease, and, these days, severe outcomes from COVID-19, are collateral damage. Because poor health more strongly affects the most vulnerable members of society, public health advocates ought to be demanding immediate, forceful government action to discourage food industry production and marketing of unhealthful products.

Ultra-processed foods are those constructed from industrially produced ingredients unavailable in home kitchens and formulated to be "addictively" delicious ("you can't eat just one"). Familiar examples are carbonated soft drinks, flavored chips, children's cereals, chicken and fish "nuggets," and products with long lists of additives.

We have the evidence: ultra-processed products promote excessive calorie intake and poor health. Many recent studies associate frequent consumption of ultra-processed foods with elevated risks of chronic disease and overall mortality. And, in what I consider to be the most important nutrition study done in decades, a clinical trial conducted in a controlled metabolic ward at the National

Institutes of Health compared the effects of consuming two nutritionally similar diets differing only in their degree of processing. The result: when study participants were offered ultra-processed diets, as opposed to diets constructed of minimally processed foods, they consumed an astonishing average of 500 more calories a day and gained commensurate amounts of weight. Participants judged the diets equally palatable and were unaware of overeating when presented with ultra-processed foods. These findings make a strong case for regulation.

History Since 1980

Centers for Disease Control and Prevention data demonstrate an increase in the prevalence of combined overweight and obesity among adults, from 47% in 1980 to 74% in 2018, and among children from 15% to 35%, with higher levels among those who are Black, Hispanic, or socioeconomically disadvantaged. We can argue about the precise cutpoints for increased health risk, but, by current body mass index standards, overweight is now normal for adults and becoming so for children.

What happened in about 1980 to promote so sharp an increase in weight gain? Genetics did not change; neither did thermodynamics. From the standpoint of thermodynamics, weight gain occurs when energy intake exceeds expenditure. Whether energy expenditure decreased significantly from 1980 on is debatable, but energy intake most definitely increased and by enough calories a day to account for the 10- to 20-pound average weight gain from 1980 to 2000. What did change was the food environment, and in ways that encouraged people to eat more food.

Food companies marketed wider availability of their products, even in places never previously permitted such as libraries, bookstores, and clothing stores, and they promoted frequent snacking (more calories). Because the cost of food is low relative to that of labor, transportation, and rent, restaurants could increase portion sizes, as could companies making ultra-processed products. Larger portions promote greater calorie intake in three ways: they provide more calories, they encourage greater calorie consumption, and they mislead people into underestimating how much they are eating. Obesity prevalence rose in parallel with increasing portion sizes.

The low prices of ultra-processed foods also encourage over-consumption. Since 1980, the prices of all foods have risen with inflation, but those of soft drinks and snacks rose much less than average, whereas fruits and vegetables became relatively more expensive. Low food prices democratize eating in fast-food and other restaurants where portions are large and more calories are consumed.

Food Industry Growth Imperatives

I attribute the causes of intensified food industry marketing since 1980 to policy shifts in three areas: agriculture, Wall Street, and food regulation. Historically, Farm Bills paid agricultural producers to leave parts of their land unplanted as a means to prevent overproduction and maintain crop prices high enough for farmers to make a living. But when Earl Butz became US Department of Agriculture Secretary in the early 1970s, he shifted policies from supply management to rewarding farmers for producing as much food as possible. Farmers responded. Between the late 1970s and 2000, the calories available in the food supply per capita—amounts produced domestically, plus imports, less exports—rose from about 3200 per day to 4000, an amount roughly twice what the population needs on average. Caloric over-abundance forced food companies to compete fiercely for sales.

Changes on Wall Street forced even greater competition. The early 1980s marked the advent of the shareholder value movement, which demanded higher and more immediate returns on investment. Never mind slow-earning blue-chip stocks; companies now had to report growth in profits every 90 days. For food companies, expanding sales in the face of 4000 calories a day per capita was a difficult challenge. To meet it, they developed new products, promoted snacking, expanded fast-food outlets, sold food in new venues, and increased portion sizes.

These efforts were supported by the antiregulatory policies of the Reagan administration, which allowed health claims on food packages and more aggressive marketing to children. Food companies increasingly targeted marketing to children, to people of low socioeconomic status, to racial minorities, and to populations in low-income countries.

In creating this "eat more" food environment, the food industry had only one goal: to increase sales. Food companies are not social service or public health agencies; they are businesses required to put stockholder earnings as their first priority. They did not intentionally promote weight gain, and they saw no reason to take responsibility for it. They could blame excessive weight gain on personal choice and externalize the substantial personal and medical costs of its consequences.

US Policy Proposals

During the 1980s and 1990s, calls for policy approaches to prevent excessive weight gain focused mainly on personal responsibility. But, in 2000, Michael Jacobson and I, recognizing the food industry's role in weight gain, recommended measures such as taxes and advertising restrictions that would improve the environment of food choice. In 2001, the Surgeon General called for obesity policies to reduce racial, ethnic, gender, and age disparities and stigma; to *encourage* food companies to provide foods and beverages in reasonable portion sizes; and *examine* its marketing practices (my emphasis).

Federal Dietary Guidelines for Americans explicitly target personal choice: they advise individuals to reduce consumption of sugar, salt, and saturated fat. The 2020 guidelines do not mention "ultra-processed" except indirectly: "Food manufacturers and retail establishments *can* support Americans . . . by providing healthy options in all the places where foods and beverages are purchased. . . . Portion sizes also *can be* reduced. . . . Food manufacturers are *encouraged* to consider the entire composition of the food or beverage, and not just individual nutrients or ingredients when developing or reformulating products" (again, my emphasis).

Since 1980, the Public Health Service Healthy People objectives for nutrition and weight status also mainly focused on personal choice but are now beginning to address the need for environmental improvements. The 2020 objectives include modest goals for increasing the proportion of schools that exclude sugar-sweetened beverages and for increasing the number of states that provide incentives to retail outlets selling foods consistent with dietary guidelines.

Current guidelines and health objectives not only ignore ultra-processed foods but also ignore three valiant but unsuccessful attempts to address the food industry's role in childhood obesity (an easier target than in adults). In 2006, the Institute of Medicine published a remarkably hard-hitting report on food marketing to children. This report thoroughly documented the adverse effects of marketing on children's food preferences, demands for branded products, eating habits, and body weight. It urged use of multiple policy approaches to prevent childhood obesity—agricultural subsidies, taxes, legislation, regulation, and nutrition education and assistance programs. It even warned that if food companies do not voluntarily stop marketing unhealthy foods to children, Congress should enact mandating legislation. But a follow-up workshop in 2013 identified only marginal improvements in food industry responses, noting that regulatory actions would face difficult political and legal barriers.

The second attempt was First Lady Michelle Obama's Let's Move! campaign to end childhood obesity within a generation, based on a 2010 report from the White House Task Force on Childhood Obesity appointed by President Obama. While the Task Force focused most of its policy recommendations on personal choice (dietary guidelines, food labels, calorie labels), it aimed several at the environment of food choice (portion sizes, school meal nutrition standards, farm-to-school programs, subsidies for healthier foods in food assistance programs, and economic incentives for fruit-and-vegetable production). "The food, beverage, and restaurant industries," the report said, "should be encouraged [that word again] to use their creativity and resources to develop or reformulate more healthful foods for children and young people."

One recommendation addressed food industry marketing. Echoing the Institute of Medicine report, the Task Force warned that if voluntary efforts to limit marketing did not yield substantial results, the Federal Communications Commission "could consider revisiting and modernizing rules." Michelle Obama reinforced this idea in an eloquent speech to the Grocery Manufacturers Association: "We need you not just to tweak around the edges, but to entirely rethink the products that you're offering, the information that you provide about these products, and how you market those products to our children."

Let's Move! did lead to improvements in school food. But its other major achievements—calorie labeling in fast-food outlets and improved food labels—addressed personal choice. The White House had no authority to force food company compliance with marketing or other public health measures that might reduce sales, and its efforts to promote even mininal regulation were consistently and effectively blocked by heavily funded, concerted opposition from the food industry.

The effectiveness of industry opposition was also evident from the third failed attempt, that of the Federal Trade Commission (FTC) to set nutrition standards for foods marketed to children. In 2009, Congress directed the FTC to establish an Interagency Working Group (IWG) to develop such standards. The IWG proposed upper limits for sugars and salt among other measures, but made them voluntary and did not require implementation for six years. Despite this generosity, the food industry viewed these proposals as far too restrictive and forced the FTC to back off from setting marketing standards.

These attempts took place before the COVID-19 pandemic exposed the increased risks posed by obesity and related chronic diseases and the disparities in their prevalence and before ultra-processed foods were recognized as a distinct category of foods and beverages. The categorical distinction is critical; it helps clarify policy needs.

An (Aspirational) Advocacy Agenda

Antismoking advocates succeeded in reducing use of cigarettes through mass-media campaigns but also by creating an environment less conducive to smoking through higher prices, smoke-free policies, warning labels, and tobacco control programs that addressed socioeconomic disparities. Strategies for curbing food industry promotion of overeating could follow this model. Changing the food environment is, of course, more complicated: we must eat to live. But taking action to reduce the wide availability and promotion of ultra-processed foods could help reduce the overall burden of diseases related to dietary practices as well as the socioeconomic disparities in these conditions. Encouraging personal choice of healthier diets is helpful but not sufficient; the food environment needs to encourage healthy choice and to discourage consumption of ultra-processed foods, especially in large portions. Let us advocate the following:

- DIETARY GUIDELINES to unambiguously state "Avoid ultra-processed foods" or at least follow the lead of the American Heart Association: "Choose minimally processed foods instead of ultra-processed foods." Note: US dietary guidelines

directly influence federal food assistance, school, and child
care feeding policies and programs.

- MASS MEDIA CAMPAIGNS to help the public recognize ultra-
  processed foods, reduce (but not necessarily eliminate) their
  consumption, and understand the food industry's role as
  a commercial determinant of poor health.

- TAXES on ultra-processed foods. Taxation of sugar-
  sweetened beverages is associated with reduced consumption and health improvements. Taxes could contribute to
  the nearly 20% reduction in sugar availability since 1999
  and to strategies to reduce the cost of healthier foods.

- WARNING LABELS on ultra-processed foods. Warnings
  about salt, sugar, saturated fat, and calories already affect
  a large percentage of these products, but recent suggestions for specific warning labels on ultra-processed foods
  deserve serious consideration.

- MARKETING RESTRICTIONS. As with cigarettes, legal
  authority is needed to consider plain packaging, curbs on
  television and social media advertising, restrictions on retail product placements, sales and service in schools and
  institutions, and other such measures, especially as directed toward children. The United Kingdom has started
  doing this, as have several countries in Latin America.
  We could too.

- PORTION SIZE RESTRICTIONS. Before the pandemic,
  restaurant and fast-food meals accounted for at least half
  of Americans' calorie intake. Mandating pre-1980 portions
  could help renormalize reasonable serving sizes.

- FARM SUBSIDIES. We should subsidize the production
  of healthy food for people and stop subsidizing feed for
  animals and fuel for automobiles.

Would policies like these stand a chance in today's political and
social context? They would confront formidable attitudinal, legal,

and legislative hurdles. In the United States, lifestyle mandates of any kind are especially fraught (witness opposition to mask wearing). Food companies design and market ultra-processed products to be widely available, appealing, and inexpensive (hence, "addictive"); people love eating them and may not be able to afford healthier foods. The normalization of overweight only expands the proportion of the population likely to resist imposed measures.

Food companies and trade associations take advantage of resistance to "nanny-state" measures. They also invoke First Amendment protections. Just as the tobacco industry used its "playbook" tactics to oppose regulation of cigarettes, the food industry has forced the government to block dietary guidelines from addressing sustainability and weakened nutritional standards for pizza, potatoes, and tomato paste in schools. In such instances, and in soda companies' willingness to spend fortunes to fight tax initiatives, the food industry has positioned itself as a prime example of how corporations can induce government to act in their—rather than in the public—interest.

These policy suggestions may seem unrealistic, but they are not impossible. Legal scholars have identified laws that could be tweaked to improve the environment of food choice, among them the Farm Bill (Pub L 115–334 [2018]) and regulations governing school nutrition standards. Even seemingly weak advocacy groups can harness their power to effect change when they share a compelling vision, organize community support, and build coalitions. Aspirational goals also have power. Unrealistic public health goals can motivate action, expand expectations, educate, and attract resources; sometimes, they can even be achieved.

While we are thinking in aspirational terms, let us not forget root causes. We must also demand policies that link agriculture to public health, keep corporate money out of politics, reduce corporate concentration, and require Wall Street to evaluate corporations on the basis of social as well as fiscal responsibility. In comparison with those challenges, taking on the food industry should be easy.

Let's get to work.

[Note: For additional reading, please see the supplemental references, available as a supplement to the online version of this article at https://ajph.org.] AJPH

TOM PHILPOTT

The FDA Is Coming for
Your Almond Milk

FROM *Mother Jones*

WHEN YOU DROP a box of almond milk into your shopping cart, or order an oat-milk latte, are you being bamboozled? That's the contention of Big Dairy, which has been pressing its friends in Congress and the US Food and Drug Administration to reserve the name "milk" for fluids extracted from the mammary glands of animals. The FDA, which regulates food labeling, appears poised to grant the industry its wish.

The argument, as the National Federation of Milk Producers put it a 2019 comment to the FDA, is that the existence of almond, etc., "milk" (as opposed to, say, "almond beverage") means that we're "being misled about the nutritional content of plant-based imitators relative to real dairy products," thereby "causing harm to our nation's children and, potentially, other consumers." As the federation argues, a cup of dairy milk, for example, contains 8 grams of protein, and the word "milk" makes consumers think they should get the same from an equal amount of almond "milk," which typically delivers just 1 gram of protein. What a ripoff, the logic goes, one that could supposedly contribute to a nutritional crisis.

Back in March, the FDA submitted a draft policy regarding the "labeling of plant-based milk alternatives" to the Office of Management and Budget, which must approve rule changes. While the document has not been made public, the FDA would likely not have filed it without intending to change the status quo. In testimony before the US Senate on April 28, commissioner Robert Califf indicated he agreed with the dairy industry's line. Consumers aren't "very equipped to deal with what's the nutritional value of non-dairy milk alternatives," he said. Asked about changing the FDA's policy on affixing the milk label to non-dairy drinks, he said: "We're moving along quickly and it's a priority to get this done, so I can assure you it will get done."

These answers must have delighted several of the assembled dairy-state senators, including Sens. Tammy Baldwin (D.-Wisc). and Mike Crapo (R.-Idaho), co-sponsors of the 2021 "Defending Against Imitations and Replacements of Yogurt, milk, and cheese to Promote Regular Intake of Dairy Everyday Act," which would force the FDA to crack down on plant-based alternative companies that were labeling their products "milk."

Others on the Hill are less impressed. In a statement to *Mother Jones*, Sen. Cory Booker (D.-N.J.) expressed surprise that the FDA would place such a priority on tweaking names of popular beverages at a time when the agency has come under scathing criticism for neglecting the food part of its mandate. Booker pointed to a blockbuster April 8 investigation by *Politico* reporter Helena Bottemiller Evich which found that "regulating food is simply not a high priority at the agency, where drugs and other medical products dominate, both in budget and bandwidth—a dynamic that's only been exacerbated during the pandemic." She added: "Over the years, the food side of FDA has been so ignored and grown so dysfunctional that even former FDA commissioners readily acknowledged problems in interviews.

An official high up in the agency essentially agreed with her critique, Bottemiller Evich reports. The agency has "too many programs and not enough resources," Janet Woodcock, FDA's principal deputy commissioner, told her, "and the mismatch is profound." As for the food division, it's "really important, but it's very under-resourced."

And yet the FDA has apparently found time to intervene on behalf of the dairy industry to deliver one of its main lobbying goals. "For too long the FDA has failed to take action to address the nutrition crisis we are facing in our country," Booker said, referring to rising levels of diet-related illnesses like Type 2 diabetes, attributed to consumption of lightly regulated ultra-processed foods. "Rather than using their regulatory authority to protect consumers, FDA instead now appears poised—in a blatant example of regulatory capture after years of dairy industry pressure—to take action solely for the purpose of protecting market share for conventional milk. I am deeply concerned by the FDA's misguided priorities, and hope that the Office of Management and Budget will return the proposed guidance to the FDA for reconsideration." The budget office declined to comment on its timeline for deciding on the FDA's proposal.

In a letter to the OMB released May 19, Booker joined forces with Sen. Mike Lee (R.-Utah) and Reps. Julia Brownley (D.-Calif.) and Nancy Mace (R.-S.C.) to make a similar plea that OMB squash any plan to crack down on the labeling of plant-based milks. They pointed to a 2017 federal court decision rejecting the dairy industry's claim that consumers can't assess the nutritional differences between dairy and non-dairy products.

For me, Big Dairy's fixation on hoarding the "milk" name is as puzzling as Califf's decision to make the topic a priority right now. Cow milk consumption has been declining for decades, since long before the almond milk surge of the early 2010s and the more recent oat milk boom. In 1945, Americans on average quaffed 45 gallons of dairy milk annually per capita, which translates to an impressive 2.3 cups daily. That turned out to be the peak preceding a long and steady downward slope. Now, 77 years later, we consume just 0.57 cups daily, and falling, nearly half of it in cereal or mixed into other beverages like coffee.

After decades as a fringe food found mainly in health food stores, dairy-free alternatives began to soar in popularity during the 21st century, and now account for 15 percent of "all dollar sales of retail milk," according to the vegan think-tank The Good Food Institute. Even so, Big Dairy can't blame the rise of alternatives for even the recent decline of milk. A 2020 study by USDA researchers found that the "increase in sales over 2013 to 2017 of plant-based options is one-fifth the size of the decrease in Americans' purchases of cow's milk." It concluded that "sales of plant-based milk alternatives are contributing to—but not a primary driver of—declining sales of cow's milk."

Nor is there evidence that America's turn away from milk as a beverage has exacted negative nutritional consequences. Dietary intake of calcium, the product's signature nutrient, steadily increased for all age groups between 1994 and 2010, a USDA study found, even as per capita milk consumption dwindled. Similarly, cow milk offers multiple times the protein of most of its plant-based rivals; but as we've turned away from it, signs of a protein deficiency in our diets have not developed.

In short, the battle over what to call the stuff we rely on to enhance coffee and cereal looks a lot like a tempest in a cappuccino cup. The FDA has more burning issues to tend to. Like, say, the current baby formula crisis. And so does the dairy industry—including the problem of chronic overproduction.

MIKE DIAGO

Tales of an Accidental Cooking Club

FROM *The Bittman Project*

LAST YEAR, I started working as a social worker at a high school in northern Westchester County, New York. As one of my extra duties, I was assigned to be a morning greeter—and I wasn't happy about it. My energy level in the morning is widely variable: If I sleep well, wake up on time, take a long hot shower, have unwrinkled clothes to put on, and eat a big breakfast with plenty of coffee, then I'm fine. If one or two of those things don't happen, I'm hungry and sluggish until lunchtime.

Being a morning greeter means I can't sneak off for coffee or hide in my basement office. I have to go out front and match the energy of the other greeters—the most energetic hype team imaginable. A woman who is 20 years older than me dances and sings; lunch ladies pass out bacon, egg, and cheese sandwiches (they learned early on to save me one); principals, security guards, and teachers deliver handshakes and fist bumps while saying things like "Girl, I love the hair!" or "Hey, was that you I saw at the game last night?" I just have this one awkward move where I swing my hands back and forth and then clap.

The girls who have their hair done stop to chat with teachers, but many kids come in disheveled, silent, hoods up, staring toward the tile floor like they wish they could burrow into it. I decided to focus on them. They have always been my specialty anyway (I've been working with teens since 2005) and they don't usually require exuberance. One morning an especially disconnected kid—we'll

call him Mateo—walked toward me and said, "Can we make chocolate chip cookies?" surprising the other greeters. A teacher approached me and told me that it was the most she'd seen anyone
engage with him in a couple of years. She said, "Whatever you are
doing is working." She knew I was seeing Mateo for mental health
counseling twice a month and she probably thought I was using
some cutting-edge therapy techniques, but the sessions were not
going well at all. He only engaged with me after I brought up the
idea of starting a cooking club during a session the day before.

In that session, Mateo was sitting hunched over with a long wisp
of black hair covering his face, meeting every question with silence
or a shrug, and, offhand, I said that I might like to start a cooking
club. He sat up, brushed his hair aside, and looked at me. I waited
in suspense like I was about to hear the first words from a coma
patient. He said in his deep monotone, "When does that start?"
I was on the hook, but so was he.

In the following weeks, he visited me daily to ask when our first
meeting would be so I had to pull something together. Dr. Daniels,
an administrator (the woman who sings and dances during the
morning greeting), agreed to give me money for groceries if I'd
mentor the boys in the group through the My Brother's Keeper
Program (MBK), a national initiative to close opportunity gaps for
Black and brown boys. I quickly rounded up eleven more during
lunchtime: a long-haired senior who would stroll in at noon to
eat with his sunglasses on, giving the security guard his signature
salute, "Que lo que?" (meaning "what's up," but also "leave me
alone"), a large table of friends and cousins from Ecuador and
Guatemala, and two shy African-American best friends who always
sat at a table in the back corner of the cafeteria playing video
games on their laptops.

On our first Tuesday evening meeting, all 12 boys showed up
to the cooking classroom. I gathered them around a prep table.
"We're going to get together every other Tuesday, listen to music,
and cook," I said. "Whatever you want to make. Just wash your hands
before we start and don't leave me to do the dishes." We made
chocolate chip cookies, Mateo's pick. As he mixed batter I caught
him smiling. Another boy played bachata music from his phone
and I showed him the old kitchen trick of putting the phone in
a metal mixing bowl for amplification. Some of the boys danced
the bachata three-step together holding hands and laughing after

putting the cookies in the oven. I couldn't believe it. Even Mateo engaged in some of the play fighting and teasing. All 12 of them had quickly turned to putty, as one does in a loud, joyous kitchen.

The group continued to meet every other Tuesday for the rest of the year. We made steak frites with herb butter, tacos de carne asada, gambas al ajillo, buffalo wings, rice and beans with tostones, arepas, gyoza, and more. I let them pick the meals most of the time, though I had to turn down some requests because of time constraints—there was a lot of interest in Gordon Ramsay's Beef Wellington (and in Gordon Ramsay in general).

Anytime somebody was late for a session, the kids asked around and sent texts until the missing kid was accounted for. They told me they came because "It's welcoming and fun," because it was "relaxing," because they liked bringing the food home to their families and because they liked preparing the dishes they'd learned at home.

Every month, as their mentor, I had to check on their grades—and it was clear that the club wasn't having much impact on academics. One kid had straight A's, but many (including Mateo), were failing, and Mr. "Que lo que?" wasn't going to class. I considered making participation contingent on attendance and grades, but by that point in the year, I had already visited too many homes to talk to kids through their bedroom doors. I didn't want to add pressure and risk chasing someone into a hole. In some cases, I was the only school staff member they were still regularly engaging with. At our school, and nationwide, mental health was the priority.

According to the CDC, in 2019, more than one in three high school students reported persistent feelings of sadness or hopelessness, and one in six reported making a suicide plan that year, an over 40 percent increase from 2009 on both counts. These problems have been steadily rising for a decade, and the pandemic exacerbated them, particularly among kids of color (both Black and Hispanic kids were at least twice as likely as white kids to have lost a primary caregiver, according to an NPR report). This past spring the *New York Times* interviewed over 150 kids—with almost no exceptions, they reported, "It's the worst it's ever been."

There are no buses in my school district. That so many students dragged themselves to school at 6 a.m. every day over steep hills carrying burdens as heavy as their backpacks, amazes me. I won't share the details of any individual cases, but they were grieving over loved ones lost to COVID, over friends lost to violence, and over family they were separated from during the immigration process; there are new arrivals every day from Ecuador and Guatemala. They were stressed, from the acculturation process, or because their parents wouldn't accept their queer identities; and exhausted, from having to work to help pay the rent. And then, there was the usual brutality of teenage social life.

I'm not saying that cooking is the solution to the nation's adolescent mental health epidemic, but a low stakes fun environment where kids can stay connected to an adult is life-saving. Authors of a CDC report from this year found that "Youth who felt connected to adults and peers at school were much less likely than those who did not to report persistent feelings of sadness or hopelessness" (35 percent vs. 53 percent); seriously consider suicide (14 percent vs. 26 percent); or attempt suicide (6 percent vs. 12 percent). "However, fewer than half (47 percent) of youth reported feeling close to people at school during the pandemic," according to the report.

Throughout the year, all 12 of the kids came to almost every session. No one fell off the radar. Teachers, assistant principals, and psychologists who hadn't seen one of them for a while could ask me to check in with them. The club was a success.

At the end of the year, Dr. Daniels gave me $600 to take them on a field trip and celebrate. I saw it as an opportunity to expose the kids to fine dining at the highest level, to have a fun memorable experience, and to show them that you don't need to look like or act like their beloved Ramsay to lead those kitchens. I reached out to Cosme, Enrique Olvera's New York restaurant which was the highest ranked American restaurant on the World's 50 Best Restaurants list at the time—a fact that would help me demonstrate its stature to the kids and Dr. Daniels. Chef de Cuisine Gustavo Garnica agreed to host us immediately. A week later I gathered white shirts and black pants from the theater department for the kids who showed up wearing sweatpants. Everyone got dressed, and the cooking club, along with Dr. Daniels, boarded a yellow school bus for the city.

That night the boys dined on endless guacamole and tostadas made from house-nixtamalized masa along with a selection of bottomless aguas frescas: amaranth horchata, avocado, jasmine and yuzu, and passion fruit and pineapple canela. They had tataki (mahi mahi) al pastor, burrata with epazote and pine nuts, soft shell crab with chile morita and avocado all before being introduced to Chef Garnica. Until that point, the dim lighting, the sexy patrons, and the swanky environment made the boys nervous and quiet, especially when they heard that Bad Bunny and the Obamas were regulars. All but one of them kept their eyes trained on the food. He was busy convincing the bartender to let him shake the cocktail shaker—(Dr. Daniels whispered "Oh my God," and gave me a frightening look when he obliged)—but when they followed Garnica through the swinging kitchen door and were met with bright lights, loud bachata music (just like in our kitchen) and a huge synchronous "Hola!" from the entire kitchen staff they felt at home.

Chef Garnica led them through each station, introducing each cook and their homeland—Honduras, Guatemala, Massachusetts. We saw the ducks hang-drying in a walk-in to produce the crispy skin for their famous duck carnitas, the chiles being processed for the sauces, the corn being nixtamalized by a team of Mexican women in a way that one of the boys recognized from his own home, and the corn-husk meringue being whipped. Garnica told the boys, "This is one of the most famous desserts in the world," adding, "You'll try it later tonight." Before we headed back to the dining room, I pulled him aside to thank him and he said, "Whatever you need: If you want to send one or two to work for a day or two, we can do that too."

Back at the table, the group became less timid. The duck carnitas came out and their moans and exclamations reached the point of being disruptive—but the server never stopped smiling and joking with them. When the giant pillows of corn husk meringue were placed in the middle of the table, the boys turned ravenous, standing up, scooping it onto their plates and into their mouths until it disappeared. Someone shouted, "It's so good!"

When we got back on the bus that night and headed home, I think we all realized that club could be about more than engagement, it could create real opportunity and inspiration, but one kid was missing. None of us had been able to convince Mateo to come.

I brought up the trip to him privately the week before and told him what a huge deal it was to go to this restaurant. He refused to come. I pushed and pried, and he said, "It's just a restaurant. Anyway, I have to work." I muttered a "coño" that I thought he didn't hear, but he smirked. Still, he didn't budge. I called his mom and we spoke to his boss so he could have the day off, but that wasn't really the problem. I had made the trip sound too grandiose and it was too much pressure for him. He came to the club because it was low-key and low stakes. I should have known that. For the last two weeks of school, I didn't see or hear from him.

The school year ended in late June, and I still hadn't heard from Mateo. I imagined myself the next year, standing at his bedroom door trying to convince him to come to school using one of my lines, "You have to jump in like you're jumping into cold water. You'll warm up." A few weeks later, he sent me a one-line email that read, "I forgot to sign-up for summer school." I called around, got him set up, and emailed him back, "No worries. You're in."

He knew that I'm not the person who handles things like that (and I was on summer vacation), but he was comfortable enough with me to reach out and ask for help. Summer is over now and he's moving on to eleventh grade. I'm confident that I'll see him walking through the doors of the building on September 1, where I'll likely still be dutifully greeting students. He might ignore me, but he'll at least show up. I hope he'll ask when cooking club starts.

WESLEY BROWN

Black Farmers in Arkansas Still Seek Justice a Century After the Elaine Massacre

FROM *Civil Eats*

EUGENE "BUTCH" FLENAUGH JR. came back home to Phillips County, Arkansas, about five years ago to care for the family's farm in the Mississippi River Delta bottomland. Today, when he looks out over the 400-plus acres that his family owns, he's often nostalgic about the stories his father told him when the entire Delta River flatland was tilled and owned by Black farmers and sharecroppers as far as the eye could see. After World War I, he says, many came back from fighting overseas and began to purchase the flood-prone land along the Mississippi River basin that white farmers thought was inferior.

The Flenaughs' property, nearby Holly Grove, and the former all-Black towns and communities date back more than two centuries. Flenaugh and every Black farmer, former sharecropper, and landowner across the Delta whisper about the missing, lost, or sham property deeds at the Phillips County Courthouse at the county seat in Helena. According to state officials, the county is one of just three in the state that don't have public online access to court and property records.

All those deeds link to the ghosts of the Elaine Massacre of 1919, which is by far the deadliest racial confrontation in Arkansas and possibly the bloodiest racial conflict in U.S. history.

The events in Elaine, almost 103 years ago, stemmed from

the state's deepest roots of white supremacy, tense race relations, and growing concerns about labor unions. In September 1919, a shooting incident that occurred at a meeting of the Progressive Farmers and Household Union—a Black-led organization that sought to improve life for Black farmers and communities in the state—escalated into mob violence by white people in Elaine and the surrounding area.

Although the exact number is unknown, estimates of the number of African Americans killed range in the hundreds. Only five white people lost their lives, according to records from the time. Even so, 12 Black men were arrested in the wake of the white-led massacre and sentenced to death for murder charges. The Elaine 12, as they came to be known, became part of a precedent-setting legal case with nearly as long an impact as the massacre itself.

Flenaugh says his family's land goes back to his great-grandfather, Cebron Johnson (Hall), who in the 1880s left more than 30,000 acres in Monroe and Phillips counties to descendants and their families just east of the former all-Black town of Holly Grove. That land, according to Butch's father, Eugene Sr., was owned by the family prior to the massacre as Black farmers emerged from slavery in the late 19th century.

"This is part of that 30,000 [acres]," says the younger Flenaugh, a well-built, 50-year-old farmer, as he looks out over property that is part forest thicket, part nature preserve, and part family graveyard.

What happened to the Johnson land is a fate that befell countless Black farms during the early 20th century: Land was taken through outright theft, intimidation, violence, and fraudulent property records, with the end result of robbing generations of Black families from the inherited wealth that comes from land ownership. And at a time when the current administration has committed to advancing racial equity, and efforts to provide debt relief to Black farmers have been stymied by racist lawsuits, the scale of violent land theft is coming to light in a powerful, galvanizing way.

A Century of Land Theft in Arkansas
Getting to the Flenaughs' plot of land in East Holly Grove confuses both Alexa and GPS. Driving 15 miles on winding Arkansas

Highway 146 takes you past the Big Slash Hunting Club, which locals call "Jurassic Park" due to the habitat's well-maintained property, state-of-the-art security, and 10-foot barbed wire fence that screams "no trespassing."

According to a recent real estate listing, the 1,650-acre preserve is up for sale for $11.1 million; that price tag includes diverse waterfowl habitats such as flooded green timber, tupelo and cypress brakes, wetland slashes, and more than 600 acres of agricultural fields.

Meanwhile, most Black farmers' experience in the region is similar to the Flenaughs'. When he first got to his family's place, Flenaugh says there was no wildlife in the area because the rice farmers adjacent to the family's property had killed off everything with pesticides. Once he stopped the white farmers from spraying the chemicals on his family's property, Flenaugh's land recovered. Today, it is brimming with life; a wide variety of waterfowl make the region part of the "Duck-Hunting Capital of the World."

"I can now walk out on my stand and see the same duck and waterfowls, big game deer, wild pigs, snakes, catfish, and other wildlife that can be found over there at Big Slash," says Flenaugh.

The novice farmer told *Civil Eats* that the legacy of the Elaine Massacre is still "thick in the air," because everyone knows that thousands of acres of land that are now in the hands of white and corporate landowners once belonged to Black farmers.

"It doesn't make any sense, because if you go look at the records over the years, they kept changing the [property] books," he says, adding that most Black families were driven off their land or "scattered" during the Red Summer of 1919.

"If you look at those records, those whose [names] were penciled out just disappeared; those that had red marks were burned on their land or in their houses. The ones that had blue check marks on them are the ones that they were after, or they just left and never came back," he says.

According to a 2019 report by the Equal Justice Initiative, the racist attacks in 1919 were widespread and targeted the 380,000 Black veterans who had just returned from the war. "Military service sparked dreams of racial equality for generations of African Americans," the report notes. However, "during the lynching era, many Black veterans were targeted for mistreatment, violence, and murder because of their race and status as veterans" and the perceived threat they posed to Jim Crow and racial subordination. The report goes on to note that "racial violence . . . reinforced a legacy of racial inequality that has never been adequately addressed and continues to be evident in the injustice and unfairness of the administration of criminal justice in America."

Flenaugh says the Elaine Massacre sent a message of intimidation that still affects the region today. And there are still some Black and white people who say the incident should not be talked about, even after a local committee dedicated a memorial to those slain during the 100-year commemoration two years ago.

"The sad part about it is that every last bit of property around here is 'heir property.' If more people understood that, they could come back and get [their] land," he says.

Yet Flenaugh's own family is still in a fight to keep all their land. Flenaugh and his father, Eugene Flenaugh Sr., and two brothers, Johnathan and Eric, had a court date this summer at the Phillips County Circuit Court in Helena-West Helena concerning a property line dispute with a white farmer seeking to plant rice on their plot.

The tense struggle has led to confrontations with the Phillips County Sheriff's Department and bad blood with the white farmer. In June, the court allowed the white farmer to plant on the disputed land, but the complaint still has not been fully settled. Larry Hicks, a Little Rock–based NAACP attorney who has taken an interest in the Flenaughs' case and the plight of Black farmers in Arkansas, said the family recently sent a letter to the court terminating the legal services of their attorney following the court hearing in late June.

For the Flenaughs, the dispute bring up memories of Elaine and the repeating patterns of stolen Black wealth. "We just want them to leave us alone," the elder Flenaugh told *Civil Eats*.

Working to Return Lands to Black Families

One month before Flenaugh's hearing, Lisa Hicks-Gilbert of Elaine entered the same Phillips County courthouse to research what happened to her relatives' land. She first learned about the massacre in 2008, while studying to be a paralegal, and discovered the book *Blood in Their Eyes*.

In hushed conversations with her grandmother, she learned

that she had a personal connection to the massacre: She was related to three of the Elaine 12, including Frank and Ed Hicks. The story goes that Frank had two families—one with his first wife, who died at an early age, and another after he remarried. Hicks-Gilbert says she is a granddaughter of one of the first sons but she has been trying to track down more information about that side of the family since her grandmother passed away in 2019, on the 100th anniversary of the massacre.

Hicks-Gilbert says she promised not to speak publicly about the massacre while her grandmother was alive. Now the caretaker of the Descendants of the Elaine Massacre Facebook group, Hicks-Gilbert is on a mission to make sure that the heirs' property belonging to Black descendants of the Elaine genocide is restored to its rightful owners.

"The biggest endeavor we are working on is creating a database of all those killed and the survivors. We're going to open it up [to the public] because we know that in finding records and talking to families, a lot of them [left town] during the massacre. They were scared," says Hicks-Gilbert.

She adds that many Black families and single men who didn't migrate to the Midwest or East stayed on as sharecroppers in Arkansas or left for states like Louisiana, Alabama, and Mississippi. Once there, they often sought out anonymity.

"I found one family that changed their last name after their grandfather escaped," says Hicks-Gilbert.

On that day at the courthouse, she learned that her great-grandfather's brother, Ed or Edd Hicks, one of the Elaine 12, lost his land to a white landowner just two months after he and the 11 other Black men were jailed and charged with murder and condemned to death by all-white juries.

Hicks-Gilbert says that seeing the deed itself helped her understand the "transgenerational trauma" she had seen in her grandmother's face every day while she was alive. "She was friends with survivors who were in the choir with her, who went to church with her, and they all shared in this tragedy," says Hicks-Gilbert, wiping tears from her eyes. "And I look at it now; it was all about surviving."

Like Flenaugh, Hicks-Gilbert says the massacre was meant to put fear in the hearts of Black farmers across the Arkansas Delta.

Hicks-Gilbert's main goal is to get an accurate count of all the Black people killed during the massacre. In tracking coverage and mentions of the incident over time, she has noticed that white newspapers have often minimized the Black death toll. At first, local law enforcement set the official number at 26. In the years afterward, however, some estimates have swelled to well over 800.

"When I get with other descendants, we're talking, and everybody's stories are syncing up, we know there were upwards of a thousand [deaths]," says Hicks-Gilbert.

She also believes the ghosts of the Elaine Massacre are responsible for the feeling that time has been standing still in Phillips County for the last 100 years. She points to the fact that it still has the state's largest Black population, but the median household income of $33,724 is 50 percent lower than the national average $67,521, and 32 percent lower than the Arkansas median. It is not only the poorest county in Arkansas but also among the poorest counties in the U.S. by household income.

Hicks-Gilbert said the Black sharecroppers that were a part of the Progressive Farmers and Household Union at Hoop Spur were not just fighting for better pay for their crops at the time. They were also banding together to buy land independently, as a path toward community and generational wealth that would have enriched the lives of many Black families in Phillips County and Arkansas.

"At least three generations of Hicks worked on the land that was stolen from my grandfather and my uncle. My brother currently lives and works near Hoop Spur, yet we have never owned any part of it," she added. "Instead, Black families throughout Phillips County were left with generations of poverty, oppression, suppression, and depression akin to slavery."

Reconnecting to Farming—and to Racial Justice

In New York City, Hazel Adams-Shango also has a connection to these Arkansas farmers and sharecroppers as the great-granddaughter of Scipio Africanus Jones, the iconic civil rights attorney now getting renewed national attention for his work defending the Elaine 12.

Adams-Shango is a budding urban farmer who began studying hydroponics at the beginning of the pandemic, after she became concerned about food security. Her interest in farming turned serious when she took a class on vertical farming at Farm.One, the crowdfunded, antiracist, and antidiscrimination urban farm in Manhattan's TriBeCa neighborhood that supplies hydroponic greens and edible flowers to many of the city's top restaurants.

"It has been calling us all this time; we just had to listen," says Adams-Shango of her farming roots. She added that her journey into urban and vertical farming brings back memories of her childhood visits to the South with her great aunt, who ran a homestead farm in Vicksburg, Mississippi.

"I would spend summers down there . . . but I had forgotten all about that," Adams-Shango recalls.

While she was learning to farm, her mother and 103-year-old aunt attended the unveiling of a life-size portrait of her famous great-grandfather. In 1923, Jones filed an appeal with the U.S. Supreme Court, arguing that the Elaine 12 were denied due process of law. After reviewing the case, the Supreme Court agreed and overturned the convictions. The precedent-setting *Moore v. Dempsey* changed the nature of the 14th Amendment's due process clause, allowing federal courts to hear and examine evidence in state criminal cases to protect defendants' constitutional rights.

For years, Adams-Shango says her mother used to share stories about the famous lawyer, but she only now understands the strong connection to farming. She is also excited about the renewed interest in his life. That interest also led Hollywood's Searchlight Pictures last year to purchase the rights for *The Defender*, a biopic about Scipio Jones.

Meanwhile, Adams-Shango is taking a leap and starting a farm with her three adult children, Kofi, Johnathan, and Hazel. After an immersion program at Hartsfield Organic Farm in Vermont, her family found a farm mentor, ordered non-GMO heirloom seeds, and made plans to pay a financial backer $1,200 a year to bootstrap a 17.5-acre plot called The Flying Buffalo.

"I think this can work, and can even do this as a family," the former Chicago Mercantile Exchange broker explains.

Advancing Racial Equity Nationwide

Returning land, or the wealth that it would have generated, to Black families poses a monumental challenge. This spring, a study out of the University of Massachusetts-Boston showed that Black farmers lost more than $326 billion worth of land during the 20th century.

Dania Francis, the lead author of the study, told *Civil Eats* that Black agricultural land ownership peaked right after the turn of the 20th century, just ahead of the Elaine Massacre and the wave of others like it. W.E.B. DuBois in 1907 estimated that Black families owned 3 million acres in 1875, 8 million in 1890, and 12 million in 1900. By 1910, African Americans had acquired more than 16 million acres. "This was the most land they would ever own in the United States; however, there was a nearly 90 percent decline in ownership from 1910 to 1997," the report states.

Francis said that total represents the most conservative estimate possible. "We don't include all the additional life-reinforcing value that having that land would create," she told *Civil Eats*. "If you are a landowner, you are more able to send your kids to college; you are more able to invest in other businesses. So, we didn't even model that in this estimate."

Francis and her team have already started the second phase of the study, which will include research on the potential wealth lost by Black farmers and their families. "We wanted to get this estimate out there first, and now there is this ability to use this land [as the baseline for calculating] capital and grow the [estimate] even bigger."

The final piece of the study, Francis acknowledged, is moving the national conversation on reparations that was reignited following George Floyd's murder forward. Francis, who co-authored an influential 2003 paper on "The Economics of Reparations," said the key takeaway from the 2022 study is that the legacy of slavery and post–Civil War state-sanctioned discrimination and ongoing institutional inequities prevented the enslaved and their descendants from benefiting from the growth of the U.S. economy.

"The work that we are doing has to be done directly in conversation with the work on reparations," Francis said. "A reparations program should be targeted to the current Black-white wealth gap as a representation of all that harm."

Francis added that it is important to have an estimate for not just Black agricultural losses but for "all the individual harms" that have impacted African Americans, including slavery, lynching, housing discrimination, and racism in the criminal justice system.

"Not that we are going to add up all those harms, but it helps provide more evidence to say, 'Look, this has dollar value,' " said Francis.

For descendants like Flenaugh, Adams-Shango, and Hicks-Gilbert—and their families and communities—that's an important step forward.

Contributors' Notes

Other Distinguished Food Writing of
2022

Contributors' Notes

WESLEY BROWN is the owner of Wesbro Communications LLC. Brown also serves as a freelance writer for several local, state, and national publications, including *Civil Eats*, the *Arkansas Advocate*, and *Arkansas Press Association*.

Most recently, Brown served as publisher of the Daily Record. He has also worked for *Tulsa World*, *Bridge News*, and Reuters, as well as radio stations and other local newspapers.

Brown serves on the boards of the Arkansas Press Association and state chapter of the Society of Professional Journalists. He also serves on the Arkansas Freedom of Information Task Force, a state-sponsored panel tasked with reviewing legislation that would amend the FOIA Act of 1967.

Brown has taught as an adjunct professor in the Central Baptist College Communications Department in Conway. He is also chairman of the Deacons' ministry at Christway Missionary Baptist Church in Little Rock, and a board director of the National Inventors Hall of Fame in Akron, Ohio, one of the nation's top STEM-focused nonprofits.

A co-founder of the Asian American Writers' Workshop in New York City, CURTIS CHIN served as the nonprofit's first executive director. He went on to write for network and cable television before transitioning to social justice documentaries. Chin has screened his films at over 600 venues in sixteen countries. He has written for CNN, *Bon Appétit*, and the *Emancipator/Boston Globe*. A graduate of the University of Michigan, Chin has received awards from ABC/Disney Television, New York Foundation for the Arts, National Endowment for the Arts, and more. His memoir, *Everything I Learned, I Learned in a Chinese Restaurant* will be published by Little, Brown in Fall 2023.

MIKE DIAGO is a high school social worker and writer from upstate New York. His work often appears on *The Bittman Project*, *Eater*, and *Fatherly*. His piece for *Eater*, "Sun, Sand, and Spaghetti," was listed as notable in last year's *Best American Food Writing* edition. When he isn't working, you can find him at a Latin lunch counter somewhere in the Greater New York area or in his backyard on Mount Beacon, cooking over a wood fire for his wife and two sons.

JENNIFER FERGESEN is a Filipino American food writer. Her ongoing project on the restaurants of the Filipino diaspora, The Global Carinderia (globalcarinderia.com), has received awards from the International Association of Culinary Professionals, the Food Writers Association of the Philippines, and others. She has an MA in creative writing from the University of California, Davis and drafted this story while in residence at the Bunnell Street Art Center in Homer, Alaska. jenniferfergesen.com

Award-winning author of the debut food narrative memoir, *KHABAAR: An Immigrant Journey of Food, Memory and Family* (University of Iowa Press, 2022), MADHUSHREE GHOSH is a 2023 TEDx San Diego Seeds of Change speaker highlighting food, immigration, social justice, and community. Her work has been nominated for Pushcart, *Best American Essays in Food Writing* as well as published in the *New York Times, LA Times, Washington Post, Vogue India, Longreads, Catapult, BOMB, The Rumpus, Writer's Digest, LA Review of Books, Guernica,* and others. She is an invited speaker to global food and literary festivals focusing on food as a social justice tool, intimate partner violence, gender pay parity, and conversations on women of color in science. Madhushree is based in San Diego, works in oncology diagnostics, and is currently working on a second narrative memoir on the Sikh immigration to California. She can be reached on social media at @writemadhushree.

LYNDSAY C. GREEN is the dining and restaurant critic at the *Detroit Free Press*. In her role, she covers the gamut of metro Detroit's food industry. Appointed in 2021, Green became the newspaper's first Black restaurant critic, bringing an unprecedented perspective to local dining criticism. In Detroit, a predominantly Black city, Green has become a voice for diners whose cultural experiences have seldom been celebrated and whose stories have largely remained untold. For her work in 2022, Green became a Pulitzer Prize finalist.

Outside of the newsroom, Green is a food sovereignty advocate. She's a founding board member of Crane Street Garden, a new urban farm aiming to provide fresh food to residents of Detroit's east side; a supporter of Keep Growing Detroit, a nonprofit organization striving to transform Detroit into a food-sovereign city; and a regular volunteer at various urban farms across the city of Detroit. At her own homestead, Green cultivates a variety of herbs, fruits, vegetables, and soon, honey from a hive she plans to install this year.

Green's published articles can be found on freep.com, and "The Green House Journal," where she shares entries on her days in the garden, is published on lyndsaycgreen.com. Follow Green on Twitter and Instagram @LadyLuff.

CAROLINE HATCHETT is a restaurant and culture writer who hails from a small town in south Georgia and lives in New York City. She's the senior editor at *Plate* and writes for *The Bitter Southerner, Washington Post, Garden & Gun, Food & Wine*, and more. She also serves on the board of the nonprofit Restaurant Workers' Community Foundation.

KHADJIAH JOHNSON is an Afro-Caribbean American poet, comedian, food media creator, and late-night TV producer from Brooklyn, New York. She's performed on nationally renowned stages such as the Apollo Theater, Madison Square Garden, Allstate Arena, and more for live audiences reaching up to eighteen thousand. You can see some of her poetry published in *HAD Magazine, Okay Donkey, The Offing*, and more. She's a Periplus 2022 finalist, a 2019 Best of Net nominee, and currently serves as a contributing writer for Black Nerd Problems and Crunchyroll. You can also catch Khadjiah on Epicurious 4 Levels, BET, and watch a couple of her produced pieces on Emmy Award–winning show *Last Week Tonight with John Oliver* (HBO). You can follow her on Twitter and Instagram @iamkdjiah, where you'll find her nerdy hot takes, anime-inspired plates, and a plethora of reality-cooking-competition screams. Khadjiah wishes to write, host, and revolutionize cooking shows and the late-night TV form.

ALICIA KENNEDY is a writer from Long Island based in San Juan, Puerto Rico. She writes a weekly newsletter on food culture, politics, and media called From the Desk of Alicia Kennedy, and is the author of *No Meat Required: The Cultural History and Culinary Future of Plant-Based Eating*.

BRIONA LAMBACK is a North American Travel Journalists Association award-winning travel journalist, Black history writer, and poet who lets her love of culture, food, and human connection take her around the world. She's a Baltimore native and former Londoner with bylines in *Condé Nast Traveler, Atlas Obscura, Fodor's Travel, Well & Good, Going*, Matador Network, PushBlack, and more.

JOHN LAST is a Canadian writer, reporter, and producer based in the north of Italy. Before moving to Italy's agricultural heartland, he wrote about intersections among history, politics, culture, and identity in the Canadian Arctic, the American South, and the Middle East. You can find more of his latest work at www.johnwlast.com.

AMY LOEFFLER is an award-winning food, life, and science writer with roots in Alexandria, Virginia. For the last 11 years she has called the rolling and verdant mountains of Southwest Virginia home, living near ancient, underground salt stores that continue to provide a vital source of nutrients and economic sustenance to modern-day communities in Appalachia. She has chronicled life science milestones for institutions of higher education and penned food-focused articles for local and regional publications including *Northern Virginia Magazine*, *Roanoke Times*, and *100 Days in Appalachia*. Nationally she has written for *Saveur* and *Whetstone Magazine*. She currently lives between Fairbanks, Alaska, and Southwest Virginia.

HUGH MERWIN is a writer and researcher living in Los Angeles, where he works on film and television projects in development. He grew up cooking in restaurant kitchens and is a former editor at *New York* magazine.

LIGAYA MISHAN writes for the *New York Times*. She has won a James Beard Award and been a finalist for the National Magazine Awards. Her essays have been selected for the Best American anthologies in Magazine, Food, and Travel Writing, and her criticism has appeared in the *New York Review of Books*, *The New Yorker*, and the *Times Book Review*. The daughter of a Filipino mother and a British father, she grew up in Honolulu, Hawai'i.

GREY MORAN is a senior reporter for *Civil Eats*, with a focus on climate change, food systems, and corporate malfeasance. Their work has also been published in *The Nation*, the *New York Times*, *The Atlantic*, *Al Jazeera*, *Grist*, *Guernica*, *Autostraddle*, and elsewhere. They live in New Orleans, in constant fear and awe of nature.

MARION NESTLE is the Paulette Goddard Professor of Nutrition, Food Studies, and Public Health at New York University and author of books about the politics of food. Her most recent book is a memoir: *Slow Cooked: An Unexpected Life in Food Politics*. She is currently working on a revised and updated edition of *What to Eat*. She blogs almost daily at foodpolitics.com.

TOM PHILPOTT is a senior research associate at the Center for a Livable Future at Johns Hopkins University, and the author of *Perilous Bounty*. He spent nearly 30 years in journalism, most recently as the former food and agriculture correspondent for *Mother Jones* (2011–2022). Over the decades, Tom has held jobs as a dishwasher, a steakhouse grill cook, a teacher of remedial math and writing at a community college, and a farmer—experiences that shape his view of food politics to this day.

JAYA SAXENA is currently the Correspondent at Eater.com. She lives in Queens with her spouse and a very loud cat. You can find out more about her at jayasaxena.com.

KATE SIBER is a freelance journalist and correspondent for *Outside* magazine based in Durango, Colorado. Her work has also appeared in the *New York Times*, the *Boston Globe*, *Men's Journal*, *National Parks*, various *National Geographic* titles, and many other magazines and newspapers. She has authored two nonfiction children's books, *National Parks of the U.S.A.* and *50 Adventures in the 50 States*. She also serves as a dharma leader for the Durango Dharma Center, where she teaches meditation classes and daylong retreats.

KAYLA STEWART is a food and travel journalist from Houston, Texas. Her work has been featured in *Gravy*, the *New York Times*, *Travel + Leisure*, *Texas Monthly*, and others. She is the co-author, with Emily Meggett, of the *New York Times* bestseller *Gullah Geechee Home Cooking: Recipes from the Matriarch of Edisto Island*, and is the co-author of a forthcoming cookbook about Black foodways in Texas with chef Christopher Williams.

DAVID STREITFELD is finishing a book about Larry McMurtry, the end of the Western and the golden age of print—the era from 1950 to 2000 when every typewriter-wielding hack took aim at the Great American Novel, the New Journalism flourished and screenplays became art. He lives on the edge of San Francisco Bay with his family and an ever-expanding library.

ANYA VON BREMZEN is one of the most accomplished food writers of her generation: the winner of three James Beard awards; and the author of six acclaimed cookbooks, among them *The New Spanish Table*, *The Greatest Dishes: Around the World in 80 Recipes*, and *Please to the Table: The Russian Cookbook* (coauthored with John Welchman). Her memoir, *Mastering the Art of Soviet Cooking*, has been translated into nineteen languages. Her newest nonfiction book is *National Dish: Around the World in Search of Food, History, and the Meaning of Home* (Penguin Press). Anya has been a contributing editor at *Travel+Leisure* and *Food & Wine*, and has written for *AFAR*, *Saveur*, *The New Yorker*, and *Foreign Policy*, among other publications. When not on the road she divides her time between New York and Istanbul.

BEE WILSON is a food writer and historian based in Cambridge, England. Her books include *Consider the Fork*, *First Bite*, and *The Way We Eat Now*. She has just written her first cookbook, *The Secret of Cooking: Recipes for an Easier Life in the Kitchen*, which was published by Norton in September 2023.

Other Distinguished Food Writing of 2022

Malia Wollan
    Game Changer, *The New York Times
    Magazine,* February 6, 2022
Jess Zimmerman
    Who Is Steven Hotdog? Or,
    Untangling the "Braided Essay,"
    Catapult, March 30, 2022
Simon Van Zuylen-Wood
    Plywood Gourmet, *New York Maga-
    zine,* October 24, 2022

ABOUT

MARINER BOOKS

MARINER BOOKS TRACES its beginnings to 1832 when William Ticknor cofounded the Old Corner Bookstore in Boston, from which he would run the legendary firm Ticknor and Fields, publisher of Ralph Waldo Emerson, Harriet Beecher Stowe, Nathaniel Hawthorne, and Henry David Thoreau. Following Ticknor's death, Henry Oscar Houghton acquired Ticknor and Fields and, in 1880, formed Houghton Mifflin, which later merged with venerable Harcourt Publishing to form Houghton Mifflin Harcourt. HarperCollins purchased HMH's trade publishing business in 2021 and reestablished their storied lists and editorial team under the name Mariner Books.

Uniting the legacies of Houghton Mifflin, Harcourt Brace, and Ticknor and Fields, Mariner Books continues one of the great traditions in American bookselling. Our imprints have introduced an incomparable roster of enduring classics, including Hawthorne's *The Scarlet Letter*, Thoreau's *Walden*, Willa Cather's *O Pioneers!*, Virginia Woolf's *To the Lighthouse*, W.E.B. Du Bois's *Black Reconstruction*, J.R.R. Tolkien's *The Lord of the Rings*, Carson McCullers's *The Heart Is a Lonely Hunter*, Ann Petry's *The Narrows*, George Orwell's *Animal Farm* and *Nineteen Eighty-Four*, Rachel Carson's *Silent Spring*, Margaret Walker's *Jubilee*, Italo Calvino's *Invisible Cities*, Alice Walker's *The Color Purple*, Margaret Atwood's *The Handmaid's Tale*, Tim O'Brien's *The Things They Carried*, Philip Roth's *The Plot Against America*, Jhumpa Lahiri's *Interpreter of Maladies*, and many others. Today Mariner Books remains proudly committed to the craft of fine publishing established nearly two centuries ago at the Old Corner Bookstore.

EXPLORE THE REST
OF THE SERIES!

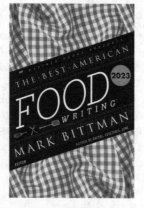

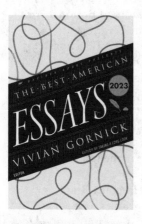

On sale 10/17/23
$18.99

bestamericanseries.com

Discover great authors, exclusive offers, and more at hc.com